**. . . a resource of student activities
to accompany the *Writers Express* handbook**

WRITE SOURCE®

GREAT SOURCE EDUCATION GROUP

a Houghton Mifflin Company
Wilmington, Massachusetts

A Few Words About the *Writers Express SkillsBook*

Before you begin . . .

The *SkillsBook* provides you with opportunities to practice editing and proofreading skills presented in the *Writers Express* handbook. The handbook contains guidelines, examples, and models to help you complete your work in the *SkillsBook*.

Each *SkillsBook* activity includes a brief introduction to the topic and examples showing how to complete that activity. You will be directed to the page numbers in the handbook for additional information and examples. The "Proofreading Activities" focus on punctuation, the mechanics of writing, usage, and spelling. The "Sentence Activities" provide practice in sentence combining and in correcting common sentence problems. The "Language Activities" highlight each of the eight parts of speech.

The Next Step

Most activities include a **Next Step** at the end of the exercise. The purpose of the Next Step is to provide ideas for follow-up work that will help you apply what you have learned in your own writing.

Authors: Pat Sebranek and Dave Kemper

Printed in the United States of America

International Standard Book Number: 0-699-47168-2 (student edition)

     5 6 7 8 9 10 -DBH- 04 03 02

International Standard Book Number: 0-699-47169-0 (teacher's edition)

     3 4 5 6 7 8 9 10 -DBH- 04 03 02 01

Table of Contents
Proofreading Activities

Using the Right Word

Sentence Activities

Sentence Basics

Sentence Combining

Sentence Problems

Sentence Variety

Language Activities

Nouns

Pronouns

Verbs

Adjectives

Adverbs

Prepositions

Interjections

Conjunctions

Parts of Speech

Proofreading Activities

Every activity in this section includes sentences that need to be checked for punctuation, mechanics, or usage. Most of the activities also include helpful handbook references. In addition, the The Next Step, which is at the end of most activities, encourages follow-up practice of certain skills.

End Punctuation 1

There are three ways to end a sentence. You may use a **period,** a **question mark,** or an **exclamation point.** (See handbook pages 377 and 387.)

Examples

Animals "talk" in many ways. ◄

Do you understand your dog's barking? ◄

It's raining cats and dogs! ◄

Directions	Put the correct end punctuation in the sentences below. You will also need to add a capital letter at the beginning of each sentence. The first sentence has been done for you.

1   *D*
    did you know that many animals have their own language ?

2   dolphins "talk" by making clicking sounds a dolphin can make as

3   many as 700 clicks in one second bees "talk" by flying in patterns

4   like dancing they tell other bees where to find flowers.

5   some animals even "speak" in ways that humans might

6   understand have you ever noticed that dogs have different barks a

7   dog barks one way when someone is at the door and another way

8   when it is hurt

9   a gorilla named Koko has gone one step further she actually

10 talks to humans she has learned a sign language when a kitten

11 bit Koko, she made signs to say, "Teeth visit gorilla." it is not the

12 way you would say it, but you know what she meant "Ouch"

The Next Step **Write a paragraph about different ways that human beings communicate with animals. Use different kinds of end punctuation in your paragraph.**

_____

_____

_____

_____

_____

_____

_____

_____

_____

_____

_____

_____

_____

_____

_____

End Punctuation 2

This workshop activity gives you more practice using end punctuation. (See handbook pages 377 and 387.)

Examples

Years ago, a cat named Napoleon became famous. ◄

Do you know why? ◄

He could predict the weather! ◄

| **Directions** | Put the correct end punctuation in the sentences below. You'll also need to add a capital letter at the beginning of each sentence. The first sentence has been done for you. |

1   Napoleon lived in Baltimore with his owner. in the summer

2   of 1930, it didn't rain for a long time one day, Napoleon's owner

3   called the newspapers and said that rain was on the way they

4   didn't believe him, but Napoleon's owner knew better Napoleon

5   was napping with one front paw stretched out and his head on

6   the floor whenever Napoleon did that, it soon began to rain

7   what do you think happened yes it poured and poured from

8   then on, the newspapers printed Napoleon's weather forecasts he

9   was right as often as the human weather forecaster don't you

10   wish you had a cat like Napoleon at your house

The Next Step   **People commonly ask questions and make comments about the weather. Write at least five sentences related to the weather. Be sure to use the correct end punctuation!**

_____

_____

_____

_____

_____

_____

_____

_____

_____

_____

_____

_____

_____

Commas in a Series 1

Commas are used between words or phrases in a series. (See handbook page 379.)

Example

I have pen pals in *Australia, Greece,* and *Ireland.*

| **Directions** | In the paragraph below, add commas between items in a series, as shown in the example above. The first sentence has been done for you. |

1 Antarctica, Europe, and Australia are the smallest continents.

2 Australia is the only country that takes up a whole continent. It

3 has many large deserts some coastal rain forests and the world's

4 largest coral reef. The reef is called the Great Barrier Reef is

5 12,000 miles long and is on the northeast coast. Australia is

6 surrounded by the Indian Ocean Coral Sea and Tasman Sea.

7 Kangaroos kookaburras and dingoes are just a few of the unusual

8 animals that live in Australia. Queensland Victoria and New

9 South Wales are three of Australia's six territories. Queensland is

10 the size of California Arizona New Mexico and Texas combined.

11 Australia has diamonds gold copper and other gems and minerals.

The Next Step Write four sentences of your own about Australia or about another country. Use commas in a series in at least two of your sentences.

_____

_____

_____

_____

_____

_____

_____

_____

_____

_____

_____

_____

_____

_____

Commas in a Series 2

Commas are used between words or phrases in a series. (See handbook page 379.)

Example

I have seen elephants *at zoos, at circuses,* and *at safari parks.* ▲   ▲

Directions **In the sentences below, add commas between items in a series, as shown in the example above. The first sentence has been done for you.**

1   You may think of elephants as huge, heavy, and clumsy, but

2   did you know that they can do some pretty amazing things?

3   Everyone knows that elephants use their trunks to hold things

4   take up water and throw dust. Siri, a zoo elephant, held a rock

5   in her trunk scratched it across the floor and made interesting

6   designs. The zookeeper gave Siri a pencil and paper, and she kept

7   drawing.

8   Elephants eat grass shrubs branches leaves bark roots and

9   fruit. Sometimes they knock trees down rip off their bark and

10   even dig up their roots. In the wild, an elephant can eat 600-800

11   pounds of food each day.

12   Elephants can be dangerous. They fight using their sharp

13   tusks long trunks and crushing feet. However, there's also an

14   intelligent protective and gentle side to elephants. One time, a

15   baby elephant got hurt. The whole herd followed the leader found

16   a park ranger's office and had the ranger follow them back to

17   help the baby elephant.

The Next Step **Now write your own story about a dog, cat, monkey, or other animal. Your story can be real or imagined. Use commas in a series in two or more of your sentences.**

_____

_____

_____

_____

_____

_____

_____

_____

_____

Commas Between Independent Clauses

Commas are used between independent clauses that are joined by words such as *and, but, or, nor, for, so,* and *yet*. (See handbook page 380.)

Example

Bats sleep all day, *but* they eat mosquitoes and other insects all night.

▲

| **Directions** | In the sentences below, add commas between independent clauses. The first sentence has been done for you. |

1 Hundreds of years ago, the whole United States was covered

2 with forests, grassy fields, and deserts, so animals lived

3 everywhere! But there are more people today and they have built

4 homes, malls, and parking lots where animals used to live.

5 Because of the changes, many animals left urbanized areas but

6 some have been able to adapt to cities and have stayed.

7 If you have a cat, put a bell on its collar or it may sneak

8 up on wild animals. Put water in a birdbath or other shallow

9 container for birds. Plant a berry bush and it will provide food

10 for wild animals. Buy a bat house at the hardware store

11 and encourage this helpful insect eater to keep your yard

12 mosquito free.

The Next Step **Have a classmate tell you about an experience he or she has had with a wild animal (not a pet). Then write a paragraph about your classmate's experience. Be sure to use commas correctly!**

_____

_____

_____

_____

_____

_____

_____

_____

_____

_____

_____

Commas to Set Off Phrases and Clauses

Commas can be used to set off long phrases and clauses that come before the main part of the sentence. (See handbook page 381.)

Example

In the last few years, most cities have developed recycling programs.

Directions | **Each sentence below starts with a long phrase or clause that modifies the rest of the sentence. Add a comma after each phrase or clause. The first sentence has been done for you.**

1. If you want to help the environment, you can recycle many things.

2. Because glass never wears out it can be recycled forever.

3. Though it's hard to believe people have been recycling glass for more than 3,000 years!

4. Because aluminum is used for many things it is recycled.

5. At most recycling stations you'll find a bin for aluminum cans.

6. Even with all the different kinds plastic can be recycled, too.

7. Before you recycle plastic you must separate the different kinds.

8. To avoid polluting the environment your parents can recycle the oil and antifreeze from their cars.

9. Because there are many uses for tires people recycle them, too.

The Next Step   **Write a letter to your school principal (or your city council) about recycling. Include at least three sentences with long introductory phrases or clauses. Be sure to use commas correctly. (See the sample business letter on handbook page 176.)**

_____

_____

_____

_____

_____

_____

_____

_____

_____

_____

_____

_____

_____

_____

Commas and Appositives

Commas are also used to set off appositives. (See handbook page 381.)

Example

Bamboo, *a tall grass,* can be used to build houses.▲   ▲

(The appositive *a tall grass* renames *bamboo.*)

| **Directions** | Add a comma before and after (if needed) each appositive in the sentences below. The first sentence has been done for you. |

1. Hogans‚ houses made of logs and mud‚ are built by the Navajo.

2. Igloos shelters made of packed snow are used by the Inuit.

3. Tepees cone-shaped tents are made from buffalo skins.

4. A tepee can easily be moved on a travois a sledlike carrier.

5. Yurts large domed tents made of skins or felt are shaped like igloos.

6. Yurts are built by people in Mongolia an area in Asia.

7. A laavu a tent much like a tepee is a shelter used in Lapland.

8. Lapland an area in northern Europe is cold and snowy.

9. In Hong Kong, some people live on sampans small houseboats.

10. The bones of mammoths mammals that are now extinct were used to build houses in the Stone Age.

Directions Add an appositive to each of the following sentences. Begin your appositive where you see the caret (∧). You may add any word or phrase you like, as long as it renames the noun that comes before it. Use commas correctly. The first one has been done for you.

1. Our teacher ∧ read a story aloud.

   Our teacher, Ms. Garrett, read a story aloud.

2. My favorite book ∧ was checked out of the library.

   _____

   _____

3. Our principal ∧ came to our class.

   _____

   _____

The Next Step **Now complete the sentences started below by adding an appositive and other words. The first one has been done for you.**

1. My favorite place *, Florida, is where my grandparents live.*

2. Our school _____

   _____

3. Our science book _____

   _____

4. My hometown _____

   _____

End Punctuation and Comma Review

Put commas and the correct end punctuation in the sentences below. Also capitalize the first letter of each sentence.

1   have you ever seen turtles the only reptiles with a shell in

2   pet shops in the streets or on logs and rocks at the edge of a

3   river or pond they were probably painted turtles or box turtles

4   some cities and towns have crossing signs that warn drivers not

5   to run over ducks geese or slow-moving turtles

6   there are many different kinds of turtles there are sea

7   turtles desert turtles snapping turtles and others sea turtles are

8   huge and they can live for 100 years in the United States desert

9   tortoises live in the deserts of the Southwest these turtles could

10   become extinct soon because cows are eating their homes they live

11   under shrubs that cows like to eat can you guess how snapping

12   turtles got their name when bothered they will try to bite

13   anything that moves so watch out snapping turtles can weigh as

14   much as 200 pounds some people like to make turtle soup using

15   these fierce-looking turtles

The Next Step **Turtles often get turned over on their backs when they try to climb up on something. They can't get right side up again unless someone helps them. Pretend that you're a turtle, and you're stuck on your back. Write a paragraph about how you feel before and after a human comes along and helps you back onto your feet. Be sure to use each of the three types of end punctuation at least once, and use commas where they are needed.**

_____

_____

_____

_____

_____

_____

_____

_____

_____

_____

_____

_____

_____

Semicolons

A **semicolon** can be used instead of a comma and a coordinating conjunction to connect two independent clauses. (See handbook page 381.)

Example

It was supposed to snow today, *but* it didn't.

It was supposed to snow today; it didn't.
▲

| **Directions** | In each sentence below, replace the comma and coordinating conjunction with a semicolon. The first sentence has been done for you. |

1. A few minutes ago, the sun was shining; yet now it's raining!

2. Todd is all wet, and Terry is, too.

3. They got caught in the rain, but I didn't.

4. They were walking home from school, and the rain started.

5. They were near my house, so they ran for our door.

6. I got home early, so I escaped the rain.

7. They're staying here, and we're doing our homework together.

8. They needed to dry off first, though, for they were getting cold.

9. I gave Todd and Terry some dry clothes, but they didn't fit.

10. They called their mom, and she brought them some clothes.

The Next Step Write three sentences that use a comma and a coordinating conjunction to connect two independent clauses. (See handbook page 435 for a list of coordinating conjunctions.) Trade papers with a partner. Rewrite each other's sentences, using a semicolon instead of the comma and conjunction.

_____

_____

_____

_____

_____

_____

_____

_____

_____

_____

_____

_____

_____

_____

Colons

A **colon** is used to introduce a list in a sentence. (See handbook page 382.)

Example

Each student could choose to make a model of one of the following: an adobe house, a tepee, or an igloo. ▲

| **Directions** | Add a colon where one is needed in each sentence below. The first sentence has been done for you. |

1. Each model must have these parts: a door or an entrance, one opening to let light in, and one opening to let smoke out.

2. For my igloo, I need these materials a cookie sheet, sugar cubes, and frosting.

3. These are the four students making adobe houses Marcia, Jamila, Josh, and Paul.

4. Real adobe is made from two ingredients mud and straw.

5. To make a model tepee, you could use the following leather, waxed paper, or felt.

6. A model log cabin could be made from these materials rolled-up construction-paper logs, gingerbread cookie-dough logs, or real sticks.

Directions Write a complete sentence that answers each question below. Use a colon in each sentence. (Do not use a colon immediately after a verb or a preposition.) The first one has been done for you.

Incorrect: My favorite pizza toppings are: cheese and sausage.
Correct: Here are my favorite pizza toppings: cheese and sausage.

1. What are your favorite pizza toppings?

The following pizza toppings are my favorites: cheese, green peppers, and pineapple.

2. What are your favorite things to do at school?

_____

_____

3. Who are the people you most admire and respect?

_____

_____

The Next Step Write two questions that call for lists. Then write your own sentence to answer each question. Be sure to use a colon in each answer.

1. _____

_____

_____

2. _____

_____

_____

Dashes

A **dash** is used to show a sudden change in thought or direction. (See handbook page 384.)

Example

Harriet the Spy—it was made into a movie— is by Louise Fitzhugh.

> **Directions** Each sentence below contains a sudden change in direction. Add dashes to show where each change begins and ends. The first sentence has been done for you.

1. Mildred D. Taylor—she wrote *Song of the Trees*—is my favorite author.

2. *Charlotte's Web* Charlotte is a spider is by E. B. White.

3. Molly's favorite story also about a spider is the one about Anansi.

4. *Little House on the Prairie* there was a TV show based on it is by Laura Ingalls Wilder.

5. *How to Eat Fried Worms* the whole book is as funny as the title is one of my favorites.

6. Yoshiko Uchida maybe you have read some of her books is a Japanese American.

The Next Step **Write two sentences about books, stories, or authors. Include a sudden change in direction in each sentence. Make sure to use dashes correctly.**

Hyphens 1

A **hyphen** is generally used to form new words beginning with the prefixes *all-*, *ex-*, *great-*, *half-*, and *self-*. (See handbook page 383.)

Example

Mom used *all-purpose* flour in her biscuits.

| **Directions** | Use each word below in a sentence you say aloud.   (Work with a partner, if your teacher allows it, and take turns saying sentences.) |

all-around	ex-champion	great-grandma	half-dollar	self-cleaning
all-school	ex-classmate	great-grandpa	half-moon	self-taught
all-star	ex-president	great-uncle	half-truth	self-winding

| **Directions** | Now choose one word from each column to use in a written sentence. Remember to use hyphens correctly. |

1. _____

_____

2. _____

_____

3. _____

_____

4. _____

_____

Hyphens 2

Certain compound words are *always* hyphenated (such as *off-season, off-key, off-limits,* and *off-white*). Other compound words are written as one word without a hyphen (*offspring, offshoot,* and *offbeat*). In other cases, hyphens are used to create single-thought adjectives (*off-the-mark* shot, *off-and-on* friendship, and *off-and-running* start).

Example

Randi got a special *two-for-one* ticket offer.
▲ ▲

| **Directions** | Replace the underlined adjectives with single-thought adjectives from the list to complete the following story. The first one has been done for you. |

below-zero	face-to-the-wind	longed-for	sound-swallowing
bone-chilling	ice-crusted	never-ending	steam-engine
cattle-herding	long-awaited	rodeo-like	storm-weary

bone-chilling
1. Despite the <u>cold</u> blizzard, today we're moving the cattle up north.

2. Clearly the <u>anticipated</u> fall move had been delayed too long.

3. Now, instead of a <u>fun</u> ride, this would be <u>windy, cold</u> work.

4. The barks of the <u>working</u> dogs were lost in the <u>roaring</u> wind.

5. The Herefords blasted through the <u>icy</u> snow.

6. The <u>very cold</u> windchill left riders with fingers growing numb.

7. <u>Steamy</u> snorts rose above the heads of the cattle.

8. The rolling North Dakota prairie disappeared into <u>endless</u> white.

9. Finally, the outlines of the <u>familiar</u> barns appeared in the distance.

10. <u>Tired</u> riders could now turn their backs to the wind and head for home.

The Next Step   **Look over the compound "off" words at the top of page 25. Write a story using as many of these words as possible.**

_____

_____

_____

_____

_____

_____

_____

_____

_____

_____

_____

_____

_____

_____

_____

_____

Apostrophes 1

Apostrophes are used in many different ways. One of the most common uses is making contractions. (See handbook page 384.)

Example

▼

You'd see penguins in Antarctica.
(You + would = You'd)

Directions   **In the following sentences, make as many contractions as you can. The first contraction has been done for you. (The number of contractions you can make is indicated in parentheses.)**

1. *It's*
   ~~It is~~ easy to get the Arctic and Antarctica mixed up. (1)

2. They are both frozen! (1)

3. But there is a way to remember which is which. (1)

4. The Arctic is an ocean that is surrounded by land, and it is at the North Pole. (2)

5. Antarctica is land that is surrounded by water, and it is at the South Pole. (2)

6. Polar bears and seals live on islands of ice in the Arctic, and they are at home there even though it is cold. (2)

7. Antarctica is even colder than the Arctic, but the penguins that live there do not seem to mind. (1)

8. Humans only visit Antarctica; they do not live there. (1)

The Next Step **Pretend you are an explorer in the Antarctic. Write a message to a friend telling her or him about your trip. Use as many contractions as you can.**

_____

_____

_____

_____

_____

_____

_____

_____

_____

_____

_____

_____

_____

_____

_____

Apostrophes 2

Apostrophes may be used to make possessives—to show ownership. (See handbook page 385.)

Example

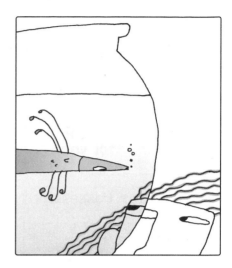

I think *Mia's* pet is the most unusual one.
(The pet belongs to Mia.)

Directions Each sentence below contains one or two possessive nouns that need an apostrophe (or an apostrophe *and* an "s"). Add what's needed to make the possessive form correct. The first sentence has been done for you.

1. Our teacher's husband is an airline pilot.

2. My oldest sisters puppy and my youngest brothers cat tease each other.

3. My fathers boss is from Singapore.

4. Aunt Doris hat flew out the window, and Moms scarf followed it.

5. Uncle Ross laughter could be heard around the block.

6. The bus tires ran over the hat and squashed it.

7. The boys soccer team played the girls soccer team.

8. At the zoo, the elephants cages are huge.

9. The snakes cages are made of glass.

10. All of my classmates art projects are on display.

The Next Step Under "Singular Possessives," write down the names of four people you know. Imagine that each person has caught a fish. Using apostrophes correctly, show that each person owns a fish. Next, think of four pairs of people, and write them under "Plural Possessives." Use apostrophes correctly to show that each pair owns a fish. (The first one in each category has been done for you.)

Singular Possessives

1. *Joe's fish* _____

2. _____

3. _____

4. _____

5. _____

Plural Possessives

1. *Joe and Rosa's fish* _____

2. _____

3. _____

4. _____

5. _____

Italics and Quotation Marks

Italics and **quotation marks** are used to punctuate titles. (See handbook pages 386 and 388.)

Examples

Some other Write Source handbooks are *Write One, Write Away,* and *Write on Track.*

I titled my poem "Singing Seashells."

| **Directions** | Add the correct punctuation to the titles in the following sentences. Use underlining in place of italics. The first sentence has been done for you. |

1. The first chapter in <u>Writers Express</u> is called "A Basic Writing Guide."

2. On page 217 there is a tall tale called Musky Mike's Big Catch.

3. I like the poem The Alley Dog on page 243 in Writers Express.

4. The chapter Writing Poems has the first stanza of a ballad called Ballad of Skull Rock.

5. My favorite story is Montgomery Mews Mysteriously on pages 210-211.

6. Owl and Highlights for Children are two magazines that publish student writing.

7. I like to read to my family out of my Guinness Book of World Records just for fun.

8. Our community newspaper is the Standard Press.

Directions   Fill in each blank below with an example title. If you don't know a title for each category, look for one.

1. Title of a magazine: _____

2. Title of a magazine article: _____

3. Title of a movie: _____

4. Title of a video: _____

5. Title of a book: _____

6. Title of a poem: _____

7. Title of a TV show: _____

8. Title of a music CD: _____

The Next Step   **Now write sentences using the titles you wrote down. (You may use more than one title in a sentence.) Make sure to punctuate the titles correctly.**

1. _____

_____

2. _____

_____

3. _____

_____

4. _____

_____

Punctuating Dialogue 1

When you talk, it's easy to tell who is saying what. You can hear each person's voice. However, when you write, you have to show when people start talking and when they stop talking. That's what **quotation marks** do. They come before and after the exact words someone says. (See handbook pages 379 and 386.)

Example

The bandleader said, "Let's have a zoo concert."

Directions	A band played a concert for some monkeys. A reporter interviewed the zookeeper about the concert. Add quotation marks where they should go. The first sentence has been done for you.

1   "Why would a band play for monkeys?" the reporter asked.

2   They wanted to see what the monkeys would do, answered

3   the zookeeper.

4   Well, did the monkeys like the music? asked the reporter.

5   They couldn't stand it, the zookeeper said. One brave chimp

6   tried to take away the bandleader's trombone to make him stop

7   playing!

8   Did he stop? asked the reporter.

9   Yes, the zookeeper said. The band changed to a slow, quiet

10   song, and the monkeys sat down.

The Next Step Think about the last time you talked to a friend or family member about music. Write down a few sentences that each of you said. You probably won't remember the exact words, but come as close as you can. Make sure to use quotation marks correctly. Remember to start a new paragraph each time you change speakers.

_____

_____

_____

_____

_____

_____

_____

_____

_____

_____

_____

_____

Punctuating Dialogue 2

Here's some practice using **quotation marks** to punctuate direct quotations. (See handbook pages 379 and 386.)

Example

▼ ▼

"Today is recycling day!" I said.

| **Directions** | Correctly punctuate the dialogue in the following sentences. The first sentence has been done for you. |

1   "Margaret, did you put out the recycling bins?" Dad asked

2   my sister.

3   No, she answered. I thought you did.

4   Me? I did it the last time, Dad said.

5   Uh-uh! I did it the last time! Margaret insisted.

6   Mom said, Why don't you both do it, and you can argue

7   while you are taking the bins to the street.

8   Very funny, said Dad as he gathered up the old newspapers.

9   Okay. I'll get the plastic and glass, Margaret said. But we

10   still have one problem.

11   I don't want to hear it, Mom said.

12   What's the problem? Dad asked Margaret.

13   Who's going to do it next time? Margaret asked.

The Next Step   **Continue the story, but now have Margaret and Dad discuss how they will get their grass clippings bagged and carted to the neighborhood recycling center. (Mom may also express an opinion or two.) Write at least four sentences. Make sure to use quotation marks and commas correctly. Start a new paragraph for each new speaker.**

_____

_____

_____

_____

_____

_____

_____

_____

_____

_____

_____

_____

_____

_____

Punctuation Review 1

Add commas, quotation marks, and apostrophes where they are needed in the following sentences. The first sentence has been done for you.

1. Mom didn't believe me when I told her that Robby has five guinea pigs, three hamsters, three cats, two rabbits, and a goose.

2. Robby was kidding you she said. Or maybe you didnt hear what he said.

3. Being very curious my mom went over to Robbys house and she saw that I was right.

4. Five guinea pigs three hamsters three cats two rabbits and a goose! she said, shaking her head. I saw it and I still couldnt believe it!

5. Robbys mom Mrs. Davison explained that their family adopts animals that need homes.

6. The guinea pigs pen and hamsters cages are in Robbys room.

7. The cats favorite place is the kitchen.

8. The rabbits hutch is in the backyard.

9. The goose Buster lives in a big cage that Mr. Davison built.

Directions   Add any needed punctuation to the sentence beginnings below. Then use your imagination to complete the sentences and the story.

1. Robbys guinea pigs are named _____

   _____

2. His hamsters names are _____

   _____

3. The cats names are _____

   _____

4. The rabbits names are _____

   _____

5. Although Mrs. Davison thinks Buster is lonely _____

   _____

   _____

   _____

   _____

   _____

   _____

Punctuation Review 2

Each sentence below needs a semicolon or colon. Add the correct punctuation mark in the correct place.

1. Yesterday, our class had Ethnic Food Day everybody brought special snacks.

2. We sampled food from four continents Asia, Africa, Europe, and North America.

3. Sue's family is from Thailand she made watermelon slushes.

4. These are the ingredients for one watermelon slush three or four ice cubes, one cup of watermelon chunks, and one or two spoonfuls of sugar.

5. First you blend the ice cubes in a blender then you add the melon and sugar.

6. Blend again until everything is mixed your tropical treat is ready!

7. You can also use any of the following fruits pineapple, oranges, lemons, or limes.

8. Vijay said kids in India love popcorn they put red pepper on it instead of salt.

9. He said that kids in Nepal eat popcorn, too they put sugar on theirs!

Directions   **Add dashes or a hyphen to each sentence below.**

1. Nutella spread it's made with chocolate is a favorite snack in Europe.

2. Kids there especially in France eat Nutella chocolate spread on bread after school.

3. Brian said chocolate sandwiches sounded like a half baked idea.

4. But Chantal she's from Paris got him to try some.

5. He said it was okay, but not his all time favorite.

6. "I'll stick with all American peanut butter and jelly," he said.

7. Chantal's dad is an ex chef.

8. He made a French snack using his great grandmother's recipe.

9. There were plenty of escargots that's French for snails for everyone.

10. Brian he's always trying to be funny said he wouldn't eat snails even if they were dipped in Nutella chocolate spread.

11. Peanut butter is a tasty, protein rich snack.

12. In Ghana that's a country in Africa people make peanut butter soup.

Mixed Review 1

This activity uses punctuation that you've seen in previous exercises. Get ready for a challenge! It includes dashes, end punctuation, italics and underlining, hyphens, colons, quotation marks, commas, and apostrophes.

> **Directions**   **Some of the punctuation has been left out of the following paragraphs. The number at the end of each line tells you how many punctuation marks need to be added to that line. Add the correct punctuation. The first line has been done for you.**

1   My brother⎯he's in sixth grade⎯and I never agree on   (2)

2   what videos to rent Last week, Peter that's my brothers   (3)

3   name wanted Addams Family Reunion. I wanted Babe: Pig   (3)

4   in the City. Finally, we agreed to get The Borrowers. We had   (2)

5   both read the book and we wanted to see if the movie was   (1)

6   as good. What do you think we discovered All the copies had   (1)

7   been rented.   (0)

8   "Now what?" my brother asked   (1)

9   I guess we get our all time favorites again I said.   (4)

10   We ended up leaving the video store with the following   (0)

11 movies Jungle 2 Jungle Fly Away Home and Space Jam   (7)

12   When our mom saw us she asked us why we didnt get   (2)

13 something we hadnt seen before. Peter and I both said,   (1)

14 "Dont ask!"   (1)

Mixed Review 2

This activity reviews seven kinds of punctuation.

Directions **Add the needed punctuation to the sentences below.**

1   Although many people dont know it Washington is the fourth

2   capital of the United States Three other cities have served as the

3   nations capital Philadelphia New York and Princeton, New Jersey

4   The current capital is named for George Washington and he

5   picked the 18 acre site for the city The White House Congress

6   and the Supreme Court are all in Washington

7   The White House hasnt always been white In 1814, British

8   soldiers burned the presidents home it was left blackened by

9   smoke After workers painted the house to cover the smoke it was

10   called the White House President Andrew Jackson his nickname

11   was Old Hickory added indoor plumbing

12   The White House has 132 rooms. The first floor rooms are

13   used for public events These famous rooms include the East Room

14   the Red Room the Green Room and the Blue Room Second floor

15   and third floor rooms are where the First Family lives The White

16   House has its own movie theater barber shop and dentists office

Capital Letters 1

The basic rules for using **capital letters** are pretty simple: Capitalize the first letter of a sentence and all proper nouns. But it's not always so simple to figure out which nouns are proper. It depends partly on the word and partly on how the word is used in the sentence. (See the rules on handbook pages 389-392.)

Example

It was a *Saturday* baseball game in *July*.
(Capitalize the first letter of a sentence and all proper nouns.)

Directions   **In the sentences below, find and change the words that should be capitalized. The first sentence has been done for you.**

1. My uncle took my brother and me to see the $\overset{S}{\cancel{S}}$t. $\overset{L}{\cancel{l}}$ouis $\overset{C}{\cancel{c}}$ardinals.

2. The game was at busch stadium in st. louis.

3. The cardinals played the cincinnati reds.

4. My uncle said there was another game on sunday.

5. My brother said he didn't think mother would let us go; she wanted us

   to go with her to springfield, illinois.

6. But I said that maybe uncle could get mom to let us go to the game

   instead.

7. Then our uncle said he'd invite mom and dad to the game, too.

8. We all had a great time, and the cardinals won 10-7.

The Next Step Write a paragraph about a game, concert, or other event you attended. (You may, instead, write about one you'd like to attend.) Include as much information as you can about when and where it was, what teams or performers you saw or would like to see, and so on. Be sure to capitalize correctly.

_____

_____

_____

_____

_____

_____

_____

_____

_____

_____

_____

Capital Letters 2

In this activity, you'll practice using more of the rules for **capitalization.** (See handbook pages 389-392.)

Example

The *Sierra Club* helps protect the environment.

(Capitalize the name of an organization.)

| **Directions** | In each sentence below, there are words or phrases that should be capitalized. **Make the needed corrections. The first sentence has been done for you.** |

1. President White, S̸enator Morgan, G̸overnor Velotti, and the governor of Oregon gave speeches.

2. Two senators, vice president Marek, and mayor Rios held a news conference in Chicago.

3. We are studying the dark ages and the middle ages.

4. Many people confuse the declaration of independence and the U.S. constitution.

5. The american red cross helped people after the earthquake.

6. My friend is south african; she speaks english with an accent.

7. In India, most people are either hindu or muslim.

8. Our school got a new xerox copier and some new apple computers.

The Next Step **Write five sentences about a historical event you have studied in school. Be sure to include the full names of the people and places involved in the event. Trade papers with a partner and check each other's capitalization.**

1. _____

_____

_____

2. _____

_____

_____

3. _____

_____

_____

4. _____

_____

_____

5. _____

_____

_____

Abbreviations

An **abbreviation** is a shorter way to write a word or phrase—a shortcut! (See handbook pages 396-397.)

Example

Dr. Wilson watches *ER* on his big-screen *TV.*
(*Dr.* is an abbreviation for *Doctor. ER* is an abbreviation for *emergency room. TV* is an abbreviation for *television.*)

Directions	Find all the words that can be abbreviated and change them to their shortened form. *Hint:* You'll find 11. The first one has been done for you.

                                          Mr.

1   Our neighbor, ~~Mister~~ Wilson, asked me to help him move his

2   television tomorrow afternoon. It's lucky I know the way to his house!

3   I won't have to use the radio detecting and ranging set I made myself.

4   After Mrs. Wilson's tomatoes got mysterious spots on them, she said

5   never to bring "that thing" near her garden again. Oh well, I'll bring

6   my portable compact disc player instead.

7   Mr. Wilson used to work for the Central Intelligence Agency in

8   Washington, District of Columbia. He's funny! His son works in a

9   hospital, so Mister Wilson calls him Doctor Wilson. But he calls me

10   Doctor Franklin, too, even though I'm only nine. Mister Wilson has

11   given me a great idea, though! I think I'll open my practice today and

12   examine Doctor Doolittle, the Wilson's cat. Here, kitty, kitty!

The Next Step **Try writing your own humorous story using as many abbreviations as you can. Exchange stories with a partner.**

_____

_____

_____

_____

_____

_____

_____

_____

_____

_____

_____

_____

_____

Plurals 1

There are many rules for making **plurals.** (See handbook pages 394-395.)

Examples

    cow ➔ cows
    box ➔ boxes
    church ➔ churches
    penny ➔ pennies

Directions   **Write the plural form of each word listed below.**

1. fox _____

2. beach _____

3. class _____

4. horse _____

5. llama _____

6. ash _____

7. address _____

8. tree _____

9. lunch _____

10. loss _____

11. spider _____

12. pony _____

13. fly _____

14. turkey _____

15. bush _____

16. day _____

17. eye _____

18. nest _____

19. book _____

20. boy _____

The Next Step Now write a short story, perhaps a tall tale, using as many of the plural words from the previous page as you can. Share your story with a classmate.

_____

_____

_____

_____

_____

_____

_____

_____

_____

_____

_____

_____

_____

_____

Plurals 2

Making plurals isn't always as simple as adding an "s" to the end of a word. Your handbook lists eight rules for making plurals. In this activity, you'll practice almost all of them. (See handbook pages 394-395.)

Examples

two *bowlfuls* of cereal

saved many *lives*

| **Directions** | Make all of the following words plural. First find the handbook rule you should use. Then follow the rule to make the plural. The first one has been done for you. |

1. lady   _ladies_   11. tomato _____

2. rush _____   12. taco _____

3. potato _____   13. mess _____

4. handful _____   14. activity _____

5. portfolio _____   15. leaf _____

6. monkey _____   16. child _____

7. wolf _____   17. chef _____

8. boss _____   18. push _____

9. baby _____   19. trouble _____

10. camera _____   20. toss _____

The Next Step   **Working in groups, think of a noun that fits each of the plural rules in your handbook. Write down at least one word for each rule; then write its plural form. (Important: Don't use any words listed in the previous exercise or in your handbook!)**

1. *Singular noun:* _____

   Plural noun: _____

2. *Singular noun:* _____

   Plural noun: _____

3. *Singular noun:* _____

   Plural noun: _____

4. *Singular noun:* _____

   Plural noun: _____

5. *Singular noun:* _____

   Plural noun: _____

6. *Singular noun:* _____

   Plural noun: _____

7. *Singular noun:* _____

   Plural noun: _____

8. *Singular noun:* _____

   Plural noun: _____

Numbers

When you use numbers in math, you always write them as numerals. But when you use **numbers** in your writing, sometimes they are written as words. This activity will help you learn when to use numerals and when to use words. (See handbook page 393.)

Examples

Thirty students rode the bus for *30* minutes.

The *21* students in my class eat lunch at *11:30* a.m.

Directions	In the sentences below, all the numbers are written as words. Some of them should be written as numerals. Open your handbook to page 393. Using the rules, find the numbers that should be written as numerals and change them. The first sentence has been done for you.

1. There are three kids in our family, and our ages are ~~nine~~, ~~eleven~~, and ~~thirteen~~.
   9   *11*
   13

2. My sister's cat had six kittens; she's selling them for three dollars each.

3. Eight people got on the bus at fourteen Main Street.

4. For homework, I did all fifteen problems on pages three through five.

5. Movie tickets cost five dollars, and we need tickets for six people.

6. On April seven, 2001, I'll be ten years old.

7. Sixteen kids in our class got one hundred percent on their spelling tests.

8. There are more than two hundred million people in the United States.

9. My dental appointment is at two this afternoon.

The Next Step **Write two sentences that use numbers correctly written as numerals, and then write two sentences that use numbers correctly written as words.**

Numerals:

1. _____

_____

_____

2. _____

_____

_____

Words:

1. _____

_____

_____

2. _____

_____

_____

Commonly Misspelled Words

Pandora is using the spelling rules from "Becoming a Better Speller" (handbook page 309) to begin four lists of commonly misspelled words. (She let them out of the box a long time ago, and they have been a plague on most writers ever since.)

| **Directions** | Use the list of spelling words beginning on handbook page 398. Add at least three words to each list below. |

Words that end in "y" and their plurals

emergency   _emergencies_

_____   _____

_____   _____

_____   _____

Words that need their final consonants doubled when adding a suffix.

getting

_____

_____

_____

Words that have the vowels "i" and "e" together

receive

_____

_____

_____

Words that end in silent "e" (often dropped before adding a suffix)

judgment

_____

_____

_____

Spelling Strategies

Here are some ways to help you remember how to spell a word. (See handbook page 307.)

Examples

Use Sayings:

PRINCIPAL - I have a **pal** in the princi**pal**.

Make Up an Acrostic (Funny Sentence):

GEOGRAPHY - **G**iraffes **e**at **o**ld, **g**reen **r**ice **a**nd **p**aint **h**ouses **y**ellow.

Use Familiar Words:

two ➜ twin
sign ➜ signature

Directions | **Follow the instructions in each of the sentences below.**

1. Make up a saying to help you remember how to spell the word "balloon."

_____

_____

_____

2. Create an acrostic for the word "courtesy."

_____

_____

3. Explain why it is easy to spell "government" when you know how to spell "govern."

_____

_____

_____

Proofreading Practice

Catching your spelling errors takes practice. Proofreading is the final review you give your writing before sharing your final copy. (See pages 398-411 in your handbook.)

Directions In the following story, label the underlined words as *C* for correct, or cross out the word and write the correct spelling above. Also circle the incorrect spellings that a spell checker would *not* catch. The first sentence has been done for you.

1 Just a few blocks from our city ~~naborhood~~ neighborhood, a stand of

2 hardwood trees separates us from the highway. When we ride our

3 bikes too the woods, we inhale the fresh heir as we get closer. A

4 massive, old oak tree stands majestically amung smaller trees,

5 bushs, and wildflowers. Its trunk is so wide around, none of us

6 can put our arms arround it! Its bark forms diffrent patterns as

7 it crawls up the tree, and the tips of its branchs reach for the

8 summar sky. We climb this tree offen, feeling its strength as we

9 sit on its enormus limbs. On a windy day, smaller branchs will

10 sudenly brake off with a crack as the leafs rustle aginst one

11 another.

Suffixes

See handbook page 309 for some basic spelling rules. Read about "silent e." Notice the exception to the rule. (You may also refer to "Checking Your Spelling" on handbook pages 398-401.)

Directions   Add the suffixes as indicated to the following words that end in *e*. The first one has been done for you.

	-ing	**-ment**
1. advertise	*advertising*	*advertisement*
2. encourage		
3. achieve		
	-able	**-ing**
4. believe		
5. advise		
6. love		
	-ive	**-ion**
7. decorate		
8. cooperate		
9. operate		

Silent Letters

Some words have letters that you do not pronounce. These are called **silent letters**.

Examples

write	ha**l**f
forei**g**n	dou**b**t
li**gh**t	**k**no**w**

Directions	Refer to "Checking Your Spelling" on handbook pages 398-401. Circle the misspelled word in each sentence. Then write the correct spelling of the word on the line. The first one has been done for you.

climbs   **1.** Joshua's cat always (clims) into open dresser drawers.

_____   **2.** After Shawn rote her letter, she drew flowers around the border.

_____   **3.** Dad stores his ice-fishing shed on an iland all summer.

_____   **4.** Glenna enjoys lisening to crickets chirping at night.

_____   **5.** Reba knew the anser to the "Question of the Day."

_____   **6.** The steaming hot coco is buried in marshmallows.

_____   **7.** Chrismas is a holiday in December.

_____   **8.** Falling leaves, apple pies, and monarch butterflies remind me of autum.

Homophones

Homophones are words that are pronounced the same but have different meanings and are spelled differently (The handbook section "Using the Right Word," pages 402-411; lists the meanings of many homophones.)

Examples

    allowed, aloud
    knight, night
    pair, pare, pear

Directions	Circle the correct choice in each set of homophones below. The first one has been done for you.

1. My *(ant,* (*aunt)* took us to the zoo to see a *(bare, bear)*.

2. We could *(hear, here)* the water gurgling in the *(creak, creek)*.

3. I bought *(ate, eight)* bolts to fix my bike, but I needed only *(for, four)*.

4. We were *(knot, not)* ready for *(hour, our)* dinner.

5. He *(knows, nose)* that his project is *(dew, do, due)* this Friday.

6. I won a first-place *(medal, metal)* for giving the *(right, write)* answer.

7. Dad *(road, rode, rowed)* the roller coaster, but Mom *(would, wood)* not go

   on it.

8. Only a few people *(no, know)* I have a cat without a *(tail, tale)*.

9. The *(weather, whether)* report called for a mild *(weak, week)*.

10. She *(knew, new)* it was her shirt because of the *(hole, whole)* in the sleeve.

Homographs

Homographs are words that are spelled the same but have different meanings.

Examples

saw (1) "a tool"
     (2) "the past tense of *see*"

pen (1) "a writing instrument"
     (2) "a fenced area for animals"

| **Directions** | Use the following homographs in two sentences. Each sentence should show a different meaning for the word. The first one has been done for you. |

1. bear   *I can't <u>bear</u> to watch this sad movie.*

         A <u>bear</u> was seen near our campsite.

2. show

3. wave

4. right

5. left

Spelling Review

Directions   In the following story, label the underlined words as *C* for correct, or cross out the word and write the correct spelling above.

1   This is a <u>wierd</u> <u>tale</u>, and I don't <u>no</u> if you will <u>beleive</u> it.

2   My mom was <u>beting</u> me that I <u>coud</u> not <u>bare</u> to <u>die</u> my <u>hare</u>,

3   when my brother suddenly <u>droped</u> <u>too</u> <u>pieces</u> of jelly-covered toast

4   on my head. The <u>to</u> different <u>jellies</u> (grape and raspberry) stuck

5   to my hair. <u>Suddenly</u>, I had this gooey, sticky, sweet stuff <u>driping</u>

6   down my neck!

7   My dad came along and looked at me <u>one</u>—<u>know</u>—<u>to</u> times!

8   He <u>razed</u> his eyebrows and plopped <u>strait</u> down into his chair.

9   <u>Since</u> <u>they're</u> were no <u>artificial</u> ingredients in the <u>jelly</u>, at

10   least I <u>coud</u> say my <u>hair</u> <u>color</u> was <u>natchral</u>! The <u>jelly</u> stained my

11   <u>hare</u>, but just for a few <u>daze</u>. So I guess I <u>one</u> that bet!

Using the Right Word 1

Your handbook lists many of the words that are commonly misused in writing. (See handbook pages 402-411.)

Examples

you're *or* **your**

It's *or* **Its**

Your friend might knock on the door and say, "Open up! **It's** me."

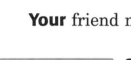

| **Directions** | Cross out any underlined word that is incorrect and write the correct form above it. Do not change a word that is correct. The first one has been done for you. |

1   The saying "It's the real McCoy" began with a man named Elijah

     who

2   McCoy, ~~that~~ was born in 1844. The <u>sun</u> of slaves, he became <u>a</u>

3   engineer. McCoy invented ways to make machines work better. He

4   invented new parts for engines, for <u>breaks</u>, and for other machines.

5   He also invented the lawn sprinkler! <u>By</u> the end of his life, McCoy had

6   no <u>fewer</u> than 50 patents for things he invented.

7   McCoy's inventions <u>maid</u> machines work so much better that no

8   <u>won</u> wanted to <u>buy</u> a machine without "the McCoy system." The

9   person selling the machine <u>would</u> say, "It's the real McCoy!" Today, we

10   use the saying to mean, "<u>Its</u> authentic!"

The Next Step **Write a sentence using each word correctly. Then trade papers with a classmate and check each other's sentences.**

1. its

_____

_____

2. it's

_____

_____

3. your

_____

_____

4. you're

_____

_____

5. their

_____

_____

6. there

_____

Using the Right Word 2

Your handbook lists many of the words that are commonly misused in writing. (See handbook pages 402-411.)

Example

know *or* **no**

No, I don't **know** anyone who dislikes ice cream.

Directions	Cross out any underlined word that is incorrect and write the correct form above it. Do not change a word that is correct. The first one has been done for you.

1   Ice cream can be eaten in a sundae ~~ore~~ *or* in cones, sodas, and shakes.

2   Their are alot of ice-cream flavors—chocolate, vanilla, cherry. Of course,

3   people eat ice cream for dessert, but sum people like it for a snack.

4   We're not sure who first maid ice cream. However, more then

5   700 years ago, Marco Polo brought a recipe for iced-milk deserts back

6   from China. Buy the eighteenth century, ice cream was a very popular

7   dessert in many capital cities of the world.

8   Than, in 1846, Nancy Johnson invented a ice-cream freezer.

9   After that, ice-cream factories seamed to open in one city after another.

10   So now we can by ice cream in stores and restaurants everywhere!

11   What is you're favorite ice-cream flavor?

The Next Step **Write five sentences that have something to do with ice cream. Use the following words correctly in the sentences.**

1. there

_____

_____

2. then

_____

_____

3. your

_____

_____

4. dessert

_____

_____

5. maid

_____

_____

Using the Right Word 3

Your handbook lists many of the words that are commonly misused in writing. (See handbook pages 402-411.)

Example

steel *or* **steal**

The team cheers when you **steal** a base.

Directions   If an underlined word is incorrect, cross out the word and write the correct form above it. Do not change a word that is correct. The first one has been done for you.

1   Getting angry can cause more trouble than ~~its~~ *it's* worth!   William

2   Kennedy learned that lesson when he <u>blue</u> his cool in a baseball game.

3   Kennedy was pitching for Brooklyn. He <u>through</u> a pitch that he

4   thought was a strike. But the umpire said it didn't <u>quiet</u> hit the strike

5   zone. Kennedy got mad and <u>threw</u> the ball at the umpire. It missed,

6   but the umpire said the ball was in play, and the base runners were

7   <u>aloud</u> to head for home plate! <u>One</u> runner scored. That single run

8   caused Brooklyn to <u>loose</u> the game. So, as you can see, <u>its</u> not <u>to</u> smart

9   to get mad. If you blow up, you could <u>lose</u> more than <u>you're</u> cool!

The Next Step   **Write a short story about a time you lost something. Use the following five words correctly in your story: *blew, threw, quiet, allowed, its.***

_____

_____

_____

_____

_____

_____

_____

_____

_____

_____

_____

_____

_____

_____

_____

_____

Using the Right Word Review

Directions Choose the correct word from each pair to fill in the blanks below.

1. Because you were sick, *(your/you're)* _____ going to have to

   make up *(your/you're)* _____ homework.

2. We walked *(threw/through)* _____ the mall, but we didn't

   (by/buy) _____ anything.

3. *(Its/It's)* _____ going to rain, so bring *(your/you're)* _____

   umbrella.

4. My parents parked *(there/their)* _____ car *(by/buy)* _____

   the gym.

5. Our class is going on *(its/it's)* _____ spring field trip tomorrow.

6. *(Your/You're)* _____ going, aren't you?

7. Terry *(threw/through)* _____ the baseball into those bushes

   over *(there/their)* _____ .

8. If we *(lose/loose)* _____ that ball, we'll have to *(by/buy)* _____

   another one.

9. The soccer team won *(its/it's)* _____ first game today.

10. *(Its/It's)* _____ getting *(to/too)* _____ dark *(to/too)* _____ see.

The Next Step **Here's a special challenge: Use the following pairs of words correctly in the same sentence. The first one has been done for you.**

1. allowed, aloud

We're not allowed to talk aloud in the library.

2. already, all ready

_____

_____

3. bring, take

_____

_____

4. your, you're

_____

_____

5. can, may

_____

_____

Sentence Activities

The activities in this section cover four important areas: (1) the basic parts, types, and kinds of sentences; (2) the methods for writing smooth-reading sentences; (3) common sentence errors; and (4) ways to add variety to sentences. Most activities contain a main practice part, in which you review, combine, or analyze sentences. In addition, The Next Step activities give you follow-up practice with certain skills.

Sentence Basics	**73**
Sentence Combining	**85**
Sentence Problems	**101**
Sentence Variety	**115**

Simple and Complete Subjects

The **simple subject** is the part of a sentence that is doing something. The **complete subject** is the simple subject and all the words that describe it. (See handbook page 412.) *Hint:* Sometimes the simple subject stands alone.

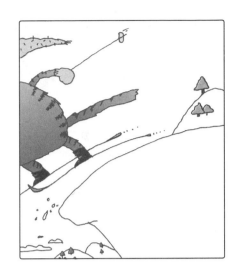

Examples

Simple Subject: Marc skis often.

Complete Subject: Marc, who loves snow, skis often.

Directions   **In each sentence below, circle the simple subject. Then underline the complete subject.**

1. Catherine visited a castle not far from Paris.

2. Roy, Catherine's friend, built a rocket out of cat-food cans.

3. Rocky, a raccoon, rode Roy's rocket to the moon.

4. A moon monster wearing a cowboy hat roared at Rocky.

5. The hungry monster ate Rocky's rocket.

6. Randy, the flying squirrel, flew Rocky back home.

7. Catherine invited Randy and Rocky to the castle for crêpes.

The Next Step   **Now, on your own paper, write three funny sentences of your own. In each sentence, circle the simple subject and underline the complete subject. Then exchange papers with a classmate and check each other's work.**

Simple and Complete Predicates

The **simple predicate** (verb) is the part of a sentence that says something about the subject. The **complete predicate** is the simple predicate and all the words that describe it. (See handbook page 413.)

Examples

Simple Predicate: My house (has) a big backyard.

Complete Predicate: My house (has) a big backyard.

> **Directions**   In each sentence below, circle the simple predicate. Then underline the complete predicate.

1. Doug is my little brother.

2. He is digging a hole in the backyard.

3. He plans to dig all the way to China.

4. He works on the hole every day.

5. Mom saw the hole last Friday.

6. She asked Doug a lot of questions.

7. He got my dad to help him on Saturday.

8. Mom laughed for a long time after that!

The Next Step Now, on your own paper, write three sentences about your own little brother or sister, or about a friend. Circle the simple predicate and underline the complete predicate in each sentence.

Compound Subjects and Verbs

You already know that every sentence needs a subject and a verb. However, a sentence may have more than one subject and more than one verb. **Compound subjects** and **compound verbs** (predicates) are explained on handbook pages 412 and 413.

Example

Jake and Mitch raise and sell guppies.

Directions Rewrite each of the following sentences two times. First change the sentence so that it has a compound subject. Then change the sentence so that it has a compound verb. Underline your subjects once and your verbs twice. The first one has been done for you.

1. Our class had a pet party.

compound subject: Our class and Mrs. Nathan's class had a pet party.

compound verb: Our class had a pet party and learned about animals.

2. Stacy held the gerbils.

compound subject: _____

_____

compound verb: _____

_____

3. Leslie baked cupcakes.

compound subject: _____

_____

compound verb: _____

_____

4. Juan brought dog biscuits and carrots.

compound subject: _____

_____

compound verb: _____

_____

The Next Step **Write one sentence using a compound subject and one sentence using a compound verb. Exchange your sentences with a classmate and check each other's work.**

compound subject:

_____

_____

compound verb:

_____

_____

Prepositional Phrases

A **prepositional phrase** includes a preposition, the object of the preposition, and any describing words that come in between. (See handbook page 434.) The prepositional phrases below describe where the cats are located.

Examples

A cat is *on top of the desk*.
(This prepositional phrase includes the compound preposition "on top of," the noun object "desk," and the adjective "the.")

Another cat is *in the middle drawer*.

The big cat is sitting *by the desk*.

One cat is *under it*.

Directions Write a prepositional phrase next to each balloon in this picture. Each phrase should tell where that balloon is located.

over the table

The Next Step Now write sentences using at least five of your prepositional phrases from the balloon picture on the previous page. Underline each prepositional phrase. The first sentence has been done for you.

1. _One balloon is floating <u>above the table</u>._

2. _____

   _____

   _____

3. _____

   _____

   _____

4. _____

   _____

   _____

5. _____

   _____

   _____

6. _____

   _____

   _____

Clauses

A **clause** is a group of related words that has both a subject and a predicate. An **independent clause** expresses a complete thought and can stand alone as a sentence. A **dependent clause** does not express a complete thought and cannot stand alone. (See handbook page 414.)

Examples

Independent Clause: Scott kicked a goal.

Dependent Clause: After Scott kicked a goal

| **Directions** | On the line before each clause, write *D* if it is a dependent clause and *I* if it is an independent clause. Add the correct end punctuation for each independent clause. The first one has been done for you. |

_____*I*_____   **1.** Something is wrong with our computer.

_____   **2.** Our class is going to a concert

_____   **3.** While you are at the library

_____   **4.** Because I have a spelling test tomorrow

_____   **5.** That Jerry wrote

_____   **6.** I called Josie

_____   **7.** Since Ray was late

_____   **8.** Until I finish my homework

_____   **9.** Let's go

_____   **10.** Can you reach that shelf

_____   **11.** That Sharon bought

Directions   Each sentence below has one independent clause and one dependent clause. Underline the independent clause, and circle the dependent clause. The first one has been done for you.

1. (Before the movie started,) I got some popcorn.

2. I got a good grade because I studied hard.

3. We stayed inside until the storm passed.

4. Whatever we do, let's get something to eat soon.

5. Yesterday my next-door neighbor gave me five old records

   that he bought when he was a teenager.

6. He also gave me a phonograph, which I need to play them.

7. If the snow doesn't stop soon, we won't have school tomorrow.

8. I ride my bike to school unless it is raining.

The Next Step   **Complete the following sentences by adding an independent clause to each dependent clause.**

1. While my parents talked to my teacher, _____

   _____

2. Because it was dark, _____

   _____

3. When the bell rang, _____

   _____

Simple, Compound, and Complex Sentences 1

Handbook page 415 explains the three types of sentences: **simple sentences, compound sentences,** and **complex sentences.**

Examples

Simple Sentence:
My beaded necklace broke.

Compound Sentence:
I picked up the beads, and Kelly restrung them.

Complex Sentence:
Kelly will restring the beads again if I find stronger string.

| **Directions** | Next to each sentence below, write *simple, compound,* or *complex.* The first sentence has been done for you. |

_____*simple*_____ **1.** Tomorrow I am going to start my book report.

_____ **2.** My best friend takes piano lessons because his parents think drums are too noisy.

_____ **3.** The gym teacher is strict, organized, and fair.

_____ **4.** My puppy has hair hanging down over her eyes, and she looks just like a dust mop.

_____ **5.** Our dog likes to eat shoes, but he won't touch my brother's smelly slippers.

_____ **6.** Tom and Mary danced around the room.

_____ **7.** The dog was friendly, playful, and smart.

Simple, Compound, and Complex Sentences 2

Learning the three types of sentences takes practice. **Simple, compound,** and **complex sentences** are explained on handbook page 415.

Examples

Simple Sentence:
I am in the fourth grade.

Compound Sentence:
I am a girl, and I like historical places.

Complex Sentence:
I know a lot about my state's capitol because I live near it.

Directions — **On the lines below, write *simple, compound,* or *complex* to identify each sentence. The first one has been done for you.**

simple   **1.** My name is Angela Zischke.

_____   **2.** I have lived in Lansing, Michigan, my whole life (10 years), and it has been a great place to live.

_____   **3.** There are a lot of fun places to visit, but my personal favorite is the capitol.

_____   **4.** The capitol is educational and fun at the same time.

_____   **5.** It has been restored and was rededicated.

_____   **6.** Now there are more historical details in the building, which makes it a lot more interesting.

_____   **7.** For instance, they have Civil War flags on the bottom floor where you look up at the dome.

_____   **8.** In the dome there are beautiful paintings of goddesses and of the past governors of our state.

Kinds of Sentences

There are four kinds of sentences. **Declarative** sentences make statements. **Imperative** sentences give commands. **Exclamatory** sentences show strong emotion. **Interrogative** sentences ask questions. (See handbook page 416.)

Examples

Declarative: The eel is slippery.

Imperative: Don't feed the fish.

Exclamatory: Look at that barracuda's teeth!

Interrogative: Do you think all sharks are dangerous?

Directions Write four sentences (one of each kind) about a favorite animal. Use the examples above as models.

Declarative:

_____

_____

Imperative:

_____

_____

Exclamatory:

_____

_____

Interrogative:

_____

_____

The Next Step Exchange sentences from the previous page with a partner. Check to see that your classmate has written an example of each kind of sentence. Then write a story about your favorite animal.

_____

_____

_____

_____

_____

_____

_____

_____

_____

_____

_____

_____

_____

_____

Sentence Combining with Key Words

Too many short, choppy sentences make your writing . . . *choppy!* To smooth it out and make it more fun to read, combine the short sentences using a key word or a series of words. (Handbook page 119 tells you how.)

Example

Short Sentences:
At our school cafeteria, I like the lasagna.
I really like the burgers.
I like the cookies.

Combined Sentence:
At our school cafeteria, I like the lasagna, burgers, and cookies.

Directions	Combine each group of sentences to make one sentence. Use a key word or a series of words. The first one has been done for you.

1. Our school cafeteria is huge. Our school cafeteria is crowded. Our school cafeteria is noisy.

   Our school cafeteria is huge, crowded, and noisy.

2. You always have to wait in a line. The line is long.

   _____

   _____

3. You're supposed to wait for your turn. You're supposed to wait quietly.

   _____

   _____

4. The three lunch ladies are nice. They are helpful. They are busy.

_____

_____

5. We had a special dessert. It was yesterday. The dessert was chocolate.

_____

_____

6. On Friday, we can choose a salad. We can choose pasta salad. We can choose lettuce salad. We can choose fruit salad.

_____

_____

7. The last school day before Thanksgiving, we have turkey. We also have dressing. We have pumpkin pie.

_____

_____

8. After lunch we help clean. We clean trays. We clean tables. We clean counters.

_____

_____

Sentence Combining with Phrases

There are many ways to combine sentences. (Handbook page 120 tells more about how to combine sentences with phrases.)

Example

Two Sentences:
Jeff wants to become a professional baseball player. He is my brother's best friend.

Combined Sentence:
Jeff, my brother's best friend, wants to become a professional baseball player.

Directions   In this activity, you'll practice combining sentences with prepositional phrases and appositive phrases. One example of each has been done for you. Notice how commas are used to set off appositive phrases. (See handbook page 120.)

1. Mr. Gonzalez is a baseball player. He is our next-door neighbor.

   Mr. Gonzalez, our next-door neighbor, is a baseball player.

2. He signed his name. He signed it on a baseball.

   He signed his name on a baseball.

3. Mrs. Fowler asked him for his autograph. She is my teacher.

   _____

   _____

4. He plays the outfield. He plays for the Texas Rangers.

   _____

   _____

5. He gave me two free tickets. They are for the last home game of the season. That was right after he moved in.

_____

_____

6. He told me to come to the dugout. He told me to come before the game.

_____

_____

The Next Step **Write a paragraph about a favorite sport or pastime. Try to use several appositive and prepositional phrases. When you finish, circle them. Share your writing with a classmate.**

_____

_____

_____

_____

_____

_____

_____

_____

Sentence Combining with Compound Subjects and Verbs

You can combine sentences by using **compound subjects and verbs.** (See handbook pages 116 and 412-413. Also see "Use Compound Subjects and Compound Verbs" on handbook page 120.)

Examples

Compound Subject:
Larry gave his speech today.
Maria gave her speech today.
<u>Larry</u> and <u>Maria</u> <u>gave</u> their speeches today.

Compound Verb:
The teacher laughed. She dropped her book.
The <u>teacher</u> <u>laughed</u> and <u>dropped</u> her book.

| **Directions** | Combine the pairs of sentences below using either a compound subject or a compound verb. In parentheses, write *CS* if you used a compound subject and *CV* if you used a compound verb. The first one has been done for you. |

1. Tim knows a lot about computers. Nasim knows a lot about computers.

 Tim and Nasim know a lot about computers. (CS)

2. Linda made a bird feeder. She hung it in her backyard.

_____

_____

3. Tracy raked the leaves. He put them in bags.

_____

_____

4. Tron called for you. Patrick called for you, too.

_____

_____

5. My shoes got wet. My socks got wet, too.

_____

_____

6. I finished my homework. I helped Jamie with his.

_____

_____

7. We went to the library. We finished our research papers.

_____

_____

8. Diana wanted to go home. Reva wanted to go home, too.

_____

_____

The Next Step **Here is a challenge! Turn to page 175 in your handbook. Carefully read the model paragraph "My Favorite Food." Choose two sentences to combine using a compound verb. Copy the sentences on your own paper and then combine them.**

Sentence Combining with Subordinating Conjunctions

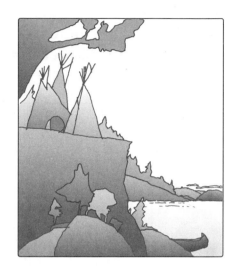

You can combine sentences to make complex sentences with one independent clause and one or more subordinate clauses. Often the subordinate clause starts with a **subordinating conjunction** (*although, because, if, since,* etc.). (See handbook page 435 and "Use Complex Sentences" on handbook page 121.)

Example

Two Sentences:
The Cherokee lived near the Great Lakes.
Other tribes pushed them off their land.

Combined Sentence:
The Cherokee lived near the Great Lakes *until* other tribes pushed them off their land.

Directions **Combine each pair of sentences below to make one complex sentence. Use the conjunction in parentheses.**

1. They moved to the Appalachian Mountains. They became the most powerful tribe in the area. (**where**)

   _____

   _____

2. In 1838-1839, U.S. troops moved the Cherokee to Oklahoma. A small group stayed in the Great Smoky Mountains. (**though**)

   _____

   _____

   _____

3. The winter march was called the Trail of Tears. Many Cherokee died on that trip. **(because)**

_____

_____

The Next Step **Write five sentences about a time you traveled some place near or far. Use a different subordinating conjunction from the following list in each of your sentences:** _after, although, because, before, if, since, though, unless, until, when, where,_ **or** _while._

1. _____

_____

2. _____

_____

3. _____

_____

4. _____

_____

5. _____

_____

Sentence Combining with Relative Pronouns

Two independent clauses can be combined with a **relative pronoun** such as *who, whose, which,* or *that.* (Handbook page 424 explains these special pronouns.)

Example

Two Sentences:
Creek Indians lived in the eastern woodlands.
Their neighbors were the Chickasaw and Yamasee tribes.

Combined Sentence:
Creek Indians, *whose* neighbors were the Chickasaw and Yamasee tribes, lived in the eastern woodlands.

Directions **Combine each pair of sentences below to make one complex sentence. Use the connecting word in parentheses.**

1. They built more than 200 villages. Villages had 30 to 60 log houses each. **(which)**

    _____

    _____

2. The Creek lived in what is now Georgia and Alabama. They were farmers. **(who)**

    _____

    _____

3. The Creek lived in villages. The villages had central plazas. **(that)**

    _____

    _____

The Next Step **For each number below, write a long sentence using the listed relative pronoun.**

1. who

_____

_____

_____

2. whose

_____

_____

_____

3. which

_____

_____

_____

4. that

_____

_____

_____

Sentence Combining with Compound Sentences

You can practice combining sentences by making **compound sentences.** (Handbook page 121 explains using compound sentences.)

Example

Two Sentences:
John wrote a story about his vacation.
It was scary.

Combined Sentence:
John wrote a story about his vacation, *and* it was scary.

Directions	On the lines below, combine each pair of sentences into one compound sentence. Use a comma and a coordinating conjunction: *and, but, or, so*, etc. (See handbook page 435.)

1. John went hiking with his uncle. He nearly stepped on a rattlesnake!

   _____

   _____

2. John knew he should back up slowly. He wanted to run.

   _____

   _____

3. John kept his cool. He slowly stepped away from the snake.

   _____

   _____

4. John says he's never going hiking again. His uncle says John
is kidding.

_____

_____

The Next Step   **Jot down four simple sentences about your last
gym class or field trip. Then exchange your work with a classmate.
Try combining each other's ideas into compound sentences.**

1. _____

_____

_____

2. _____

_____

_____

3. _____

_____

_____

4. _____

_____

Sentence Combining Review 1

It's time to review all the different ways you've learned to combine sentences.

Directions   **Combine each set of sentences below into a longer, smoother sentence.**

1. The ancient Greeks thought Poseidon caused earthquakes. He was their sea god. (Use an appositive phrase.)

_____

_____

2. The Japanese said quakes were caused by a huge catfish. It lived under the earth. (Use a subordinate clause starting with *that.*)

_____

_____

3. Scientists discovered the true cause of earthquakes. They discovered it recently. (Use a key word.)

_____

_____

4. The earth's crust moves. Land masses bump together. (Use *and* to make a compound sentence.)

_____

_____

5. This causes shaking. It causes buckling. It causes cracking. (Use a series of words.)

_____

6. Bears can predict earthquakes. Other animals can, too.
(Use a compound subject.)

_____

_____

7. Bears usually hibernate all winter. The bears in a Japanese zoo suddenly woke up before one earthquake.
(Make a compound sentence.)

_____

_____

8. They woke up early and began pacing. They paced around their cage.
(Use a prepositional phrase.)

_____

_____

The Next Step   **Write two short sentences about earthquakes. Your sentences can be serious or silly. Trade papers with a partner and combine each other's sentences.**

_____

_____

_____

_____

_____

Sentence Combining Review 2

Here's your chance to show off your sentence-combining skills.

Directions **Rewrite the following paragraph. Use what you have learned about sentence combining to make it read more smoothly. The first combination has been done for you.**

Everyone knows that the oceans provide fish. They provide many other products, too. For example, oceans provide seaweed. The Japanese use seaweed in cooking. The Irish use seaweed in cooking, too. Seaweed is also used to make paint. It is used to make toothpaste. It is even used to make ice cream. Oceans provide salt. Salt is made from seawater—another name for ocean water. This is done in China. Oceans also provide coral. Coral is used to make jewelry. Coral is found in shallow water.

Everyone knows that the oceans provide fish, but they provide

many other products, too.

_____

_____

_____

_____

_____

_____

| Directions | Now try it again. Combine some of the sentences to make the following paragraph read more smoothly. |

The seas are filled with fish. They are also swimming with stories. There are stories about dragons. The dragons have two heads. There are tales about pirates. There are tales about sunken treasure. There are tales about ghost ships. One ghost ship was named the *Mary Celeste*. All its passengers disappeared at sea. This happened in 1872. They were never found. Herman Melville wrote a sea story. It is famous. It is about Moby Dick. Moby Dick is a whale. He is huge.

_____

_____

_____

_____

_____

_____

_____

The Next Step **Choose one of the following: (1) Write a few more smooth, interesting sentences to finish the paragraph above. (2) On your own paper, tell a sea story you know, or make one up!**

Fragments 1

Your handbook explains several kinds of sentence errors and how to correct them. (See handbook page 115.) This activity gives you practice correcting one kind of sentence error: **sentence fragments.**

Example

Fragment:
The Aztecs in what is now Mexico.

Sentence:
The Aztecs *lived* in what is now Mexico.

Directions   On each line below, put an *S* if the words that follow make a sentence. Put an *F* if they make a sentence fragment. The first one has been marked for you. (There are seven fragments.)

_____*S*_____   **1.** They built cities during the 1200s.

_____   **2.** Within their main city, parks and a zoo.

_____   **3.** The Aztecs used chocolate as money.

_____   **4.** Also traded with gold, copper, and cloth.

_____   **5.** The Maya in Central America.

_____   **6.** Built the tallest pyramid in the New World.

_____   **7.** A kind of picture writing called hieroglyphics.

_____   **8.** Wrote on bark paper.

_____   **9.** The Incas lived in South America.

_____   **10.** They lived in the Andes Mountains.

_____   **11.** Built 12,000 miles of roads and huge buildings.

The Next Step **Go back to the fragments on page 101 and add words to make them complete sentences. The first one has been done for you.**

1. __Within their main city, the Aztecs created parks and a zoo.__

_____

2. _____

_____

3. _____

_____

4. _____

_____

5. _____

_____

6. _____

_____

7. _____

_____

Fragments 2

In this activity, you will practice correcting **sentence fragments.** (See handbook page 115.)

Example

Fragment:
The Inuit people in the Arctic.

Sentence:
The Inuit people *live* in the Arctic.

Directions On each line below, put an *S* if the words that follow make a sentence. Put an *F* if they make a sentence fragment. The first one has been marked for you. (There are eight fragments.)

___F___ **1.** Called the Inuit "Eskimos."

_____ **2.** The word "Inuit" means "the people."

_____ **3.** Some Inuit used to live in igloos in the winter.

_____ **4.** Igloos were made out of blocks of ice and snow.

_____ **5.** Clear ice blocks for windows.

_____ **6.** Others huts out of whale bones.

_____ **7.** Also made one-person boats called "kayaks."

_____ **8.** Larger boats called "umiaks."

_____ **9.** Made sleds that were pulled by dogs.

_____ **10.** The Inuit people have a proud tradition.

_____ **11.** Now live in pre-built houses.

_____ **12.** Use snowmobiles.

The Next Step   **Using the fragments on page 103, add words to make them complete sentences. The first one has been done for you.**

1. *Explorers called the Inuit "Eskimos."*

2. _____

    _____

3. _____

    _____

4. _____

    _____

5. _____

    _____

6. _____

    _____

7. _____

    _____

8. _____

    _____

Run-On Sentences 1

Your handbook explains a kind of sentence error called **run-on sentences** and tells you how to correct them. (See handbook page 115.)

Example

Run-On Sentence:
A fish never shuts its eyes it can't even blink.

Corrected Sentence:
A fish never shuts its eyes. It can't even blink.
(Add end punctuation and a capital letter to make two sentences.)

Directions   Correct the run-on sentences below by dividing them into two sentences. Use correct capitalization and end punctuation in your new sentences. The first one has been done for you.

1. Earthworms have 10 hearts. Snails have eyes on their feelers.

2. Grasshoppers can jump 30 inches that's like you jumping a football field.

3. Ants can lift 50 times their weight how much can you lift?

4. Squirrels bury more nuts than they dig up the nuts left in the ground sometimes grow into trees.

5. Birds' wings are made of feathers bats' wings are made of skin.

6. Camels drink as much as 30 gallons of water at one time no wonder they can cross deserts.

7. Kangaroo rats never drink water they get the water they need from the plants they eat.

The Next Step **Write three run-on sentences about animals. Exchange papers with a classmate and correct each other's run-ons by dividing them into separate sentences.**

Run-On Sentences:

1. _____

_____

2. _____

_____

3. _____

_____

Corrected Sentences:

1. _____

_____

_____

2. _____

_____

_____

3. _____

_____

_____

Run-On Sentences 2

In this activity, you'll practice correcting **run-on sentences** by adding a comma and a coordinating conjunction. Here are some conjunctions to choose from: *and, but, so,* and *yet.* (See handbook page 380.)

Example

Run-On Sentence:
Panda bears live in China they eat bamboo.

Corrected Sentence:
Panda bears live in China, *and* they eat bamboo.

Directions	Correct the run-on sentences below by adding a comma and a conjunction. The first one has been done for you.

1. There are eight basic kinds of bears, *and* the "big brown bears" are the largest bears in the world.

2. "Sun bears" are the smallest kind of bear they weigh 60 to 100 pounds.

3. "Polar bears," a third kind, live in the Arctic they go swimming in very cold water.

4. Their thick fur keeps them warm their front paws work as paddles.

5. "Grizzly bears," a fourth kind of bear, used to roam freely in the West now most of them live in national parks.

6. There are "American black bears," "Asiatic black bears," and "spectacled bears" don't forget the slow-moving "sloth bears."

7. A bear travels over a large area during the summer in the winter it stays in a warm den.

8. Bears can run faster than people only black bears can climb trees.

The Next Step Write a story about bears or another animal of your choice. Try to use at least two sentences that include a comma and a conjunction such as *and, but, so, or,* and *yet.*

_____

_____

_____

_____

_____

_____

_____

_____

_____

_____

Rambling Sentences

In this activity, you'll practice correcting another kind of sentence error: the **rambling sentence.** (See handbook page 115.)

Example

Rambling Sentence:
I got up in a hurry and I ate my cereal and then I got on the school bus and I saw my best friend.

Corrected Sentences:
I got up in a hurry and ate my cereal. Then I got on the school bus and saw my best friend.

 **Directions** Read the two rambling sentences below. Correct them by dividing them into as many sentences as you think are needed. Cross out the extra *and*'s, capitalize the first letter of each sentence, and use correct end punctuation. The first line has been done for you.

1. Misha and I went to the zoo yesterday. ~~and~~ **W**e saw polar bears,

   zebras, and elephants and we also saw seals and otters and then

   we got some ice cream and rested for a few minutes and finally,

   we saw the baby animals in the children's zoo and the little

   llamas were the friendliest babies.

2. My mom went to Japan on a business trip and she called me as

   soon as she got there and she said it was already Wednesday

   there even though it was only Tuesday here and I asked her how

   she could be in a different day and still be talking to me and she

   said I should ask my science teacher.

The Next Step **Write a short story about an unusual lunch time. Use *and*'s instead of end punctuation so that you have one long rambling sentence. Exchange papers with a classmate and correct each other's rambling sentence.**

_____

_____

_____

_____

_____

_____

_____

_____

_____

_____

_____

_____

_____

Sentence Problems

Certain problems can sneak into your sentences right under your nose! Some of these problems are explained on handbook page 117.

Example

Double Subject:
My brother Mark *he* loves ice cream.

Corrected Sentence:
My brother Mark loves ice cream.

Directions **Each of the following sentences contains one of the problems discussed on page 117 in your handbook. Correct each sentence by crossing out or changing the problem word. The first one has been done for you.**

1. My mom ~~she~~ only lets Mark have ice cream after dinner.

2. He doesn't get no ice cream unless he eats all of his dinner.

3. He begs, but Mom says he should of eaten his vegetables.

4. He'll say, "Harley doesn't have to eat no vegetables!"

5. Harley he's our dog.

6. "Harley doesn't get no ice cream, either!" Mom says.

7. I could of told her that Harley did get ice cream once.

8. Mark he gave it to Harley when no one was watching.

9. Dogs shouldn't eat no chocolate, so Mark gave Harley strawberry.

10. If Mark and Harley could get away with it, he would eat gallons and

    gallons of ice cream.

The Next Step Write three more sentences about Mark and Harley. Be careful to avoid the sentence problems you corrected on the previous page.

_____

_____

_____

_____

_____

_____

_____

_____

_____

_____

_____

_____

_____

_____

_____

Sentence Problems Review

In this activity, you will practice correcting many of the sentence errors you have learned about.

Directions **The following paragraph contains sentence fragments, run-on sentences, and other problems. Make each sentence complete and correct. The first correction has been done for you.**

But if you do, you are

1   You may think that dragons live only in fairy tales. ⋀W̶rong.

2   Really do exist. Komodo dragons they are huge lizards. They can

3   grow to be 10 feet long and weigh as much as 300 pounds. Like

4   other reptiles, lay eggs. Although they are big and heavy, Komodo

5   dragons can run very fast. These lizards can catch small deer,

6   wild pigs, and other small animals, his bite is deadly. Don't never

7   have to worry about being bitten by a Komodo dragon unless you

8   live in Indonesia that's where the dragons live. If you would like

9   to see one up close and in person, just go to Komodo Island

10   National Park about 1,000 dragons there.

Directions	The paragraph below contains run-on and rambling sentences. Correct them by breaking them into shorter sentences. The first one has been done for you.

1   There are many types of lizards besides Komodo dragon~~s~~.

2   **S**
     ~~s~~ome of them live in the United States and one type of lizard

3   that lives in this country is the Gila monster it is poisonous, and

4   it grows as long as two feet. Gila monsters are slow-moving

5   lizards that live in the desert Southwest and they eat eggs, birds,

6   and rodents and they store fat in their tails so they can live for

7   months without food if they have to. The bite of a Gila monster

8   hurts, but it would not kill a person. Of course there are many

9   kinds of lizards that are harmless and some people even keep

10   lizards as pets and my friend Emily puts her iguana on a leash

11   and takes it everywhere with her. Unlike most other lizards,

12   iguanas eat plants, fruit, and flowers.

Changing Sentence Beginnings

When you proofread your writing, you may find that too many of your sentences start with the same word. (Check out "Change Sentence Beginnings" on handbook page 65.)

Example

We went to the beach on Saturday.

On Saturday we went to the beach.

(Now the sentence starts with a phrase instead of *we*.)

Directions | **Rewrite the following sentences, giving each a different beginning. The first one has been done for you.**

1. We took a big umbrella to keep from getting sunburned.

   To keep from getting sunburned, we took a big umbrella.

2. We took sandwiches for lunch.

   _____

3. We all went into the water as soon as we got there.

   _____

4. We played catch after we ate lunch.

   _____

5. We had to quit when our ball got lost in the ocean.

   _____

6. We were all tired by the time we got home.

   _____

The Next Step Write a short, personal narrative (true story about yourself) about a day at the beach, pool, or park. Then pick two sentences from your story and change the way they begin.

_____

_____

_____

_____

_____

_____

_____

_____

New Sentences:

1. _____

_____

_____

2. _____

_____

_____

Using Powerful Verbs and Specific Nouns

When you polish your writing, make sure to use powerful verbs and specific nouns. (Handbook page 66 gives some examples.)

Examples

Our class *pet* is named Barney.

With a Specific Noun:
Our class *guinea pig* is named Barney.

Directions   **In the sentences below, replace the nouns in parentheses with nouns that are more specific. Replace the verbs with verbs that are more powerful. The first sentence has been done for you.**

1. The teacher *(told)* _____ *ordered* _____ Josh to put Barney back

   in his cage.

2. My mom keeps a *(container)* _____ of

   (fruit) _____ on the kitchen counter.

3. The *(dog)* _____ from across the street

   (went) _____ after the ball.

4. Yesterday, a *(man)* _____ with an old hat

   (came) _____ into the room.

5. We played *(a game)* _____ and watched

   (a TV show) _____ .

6. The woman behind me at the movie was *(talking)* _____ .

7. Every summer my *(relative)* _____ grows

(vegetables) _____ .

8. Dad asked me to *(go)* _____ to the store to pick up

some *(food)* _____ .

The Next Step **Using the newspaper headline below as your starting point, write the first draft of a news story. Use specific nouns and powerful verbs in your story.**

Flying Saucer Lands on Playground

_____

_____

_____

_____

_____

_____

_____

_____

_____

Language Activities

Every activity in this section includes a main practice part in which you learn about or review the different parts of speech. Most of the activities also include helpful handbook references. In addition, The Next Step, which is at the end of most activities, encourages follow-up practice of certain skills.

Nouns

A **noun** names a person, a place, a thing, or an idea. (See handbook page 418.)

Examples

A Person: aquanaut

A Place: Mariana Trench

A Thing: bathysphere

An Idea: oceanography

Directions	Circle all the nouns in the sentences below. The number after each sentence tells you how many nouns it has. The first sentence has been done for you.

1. I was so surprised you could have knocked me over with a (feather.) (1)

2. Don't sit there like a bump on a log. (2)

3. That boy is barking up the wrong tree. (2)

4. It's all water under the bridge. (2)

5. Rome wasn't built in a day. (2)

6. The doctors x-rayed my head and found nothing wrong. (3)

7. This is the greatest city in America. (2)

8. Forgetfulness is my biggest weakness. (2)

9. Don't miss tomorrow's game. (1)

10. Let's hope Steve gets his curveball working. (2)

The Next Step **Reread the sentences in the previous exercise. Write some sayings that you know. Circle all the nouns in your sentences.**

1. _____

_____

_____

2. _____

_____

_____

3. _____

_____

_____

4. _____

_____

_____

5. _____

_____

_____

Common and Proper Nouns

A **common noun** is the *general* name of a person, a place, a thing, or an idea. A **proper noun** is a *particular* name of a person, a place, a thing, or an idea. Remember to use capital letters for proper nouns. (See handbook page 418.)

Examples

> *Common Nouns:* man, woman
>
> *Proper Nouns:* Mr. Thun, Ms. Felipe

Directions   Write a common noun to go with each proper noun. Then write a proper noun to go with each common noun.

Proper Nouns	Common Nouns
1. Milwaukee	_____
2. Florida	_____
3. Pacific	_____
4. Sunday	_____
5. October	_____
6. _____	boy
7. _____	river
8. _____	team
9. _____	athlete
10. _____	school

The Next Step **Now write five sentences. Use a common and a proper noun in each one. Mark each common noun with a *C* and each proper noun with a *P*.**

Example

      P   C

Washington was our first president.

1. _____

_____

_____

2. _____

_____

_____

3. _____

_____

_____

4. _____

_____

_____

5. _____

_____

_____

Singular and Plural Nouns

A **singular noun** names one person, place, thing, or idea. A **plural noun** names more than one person, place, thing, or idea. (See handbook page 418.)

Examples

Singular Nouns:	marker	shoe	student
Plural Nouns:	markers	shoes	students

Directions | Write a humorous paragraph about a recent school activity. To get started, you might want to use some of the words above. When you are finished, mark each plural noun with a *P* and each singular noun with an *S.*

_____

_____

_____

_____

_____

_____

_____

_____

Using Nouns

A **subject noun** is a noun that does something or is being talked about. A **predicate noun** is a noun that renames the subject. A predicate noun is linked to the subject by a linking verb. A **possessive noun** is a noun used to show possession or ownership. (See handbook page 420.)

Directions   Write your own sentences below. Use the sentences on handbook page 420 as models.

Use subject nouns. **Underline and label them (SN).**

1. _____

_____

2. _____

_____

Use predicate nouns. **Underline and label them (PN).**

1. _____

_____

2. _____

_____

Use possessive nouns. **Underline and label them (POS).**

1. _____

_____

2. _____

_____

Concrete and Abstract Nouns

Concrete nouns name things that can be touched or seen. **Abstract nouns** name things that cannot be touched or seen. (See handbook page 418.)

Examples

Concrete Nouns: shoe, building, sky, Ohio

Abstract Nouns: mystery, laziness, fear

Directions Sort the nouns below into two groups: concrete and abstract nouns. Write each noun in the correct column.

tractor	strength	lamp	sadness
students	health	hope	lawn
zoo	eye	thought	computer
idea	supermarket	sun	software

Concrete Nouns	Abstract Nouns

Directions Now think of three more nouns to add to each column. If you need ideas, skim your handbook or look around you! Things you can see are concrete nouns. Moods, feelings, ideas, and so on, are abstract nouns.

Concrete Nouns   **Abstract Nouns**

_____   _____

_____   _____

_____   _____

The Next Step **Write three sentences using one concrete noun and one abstract noun. Circle the nouns. An example has been done for you.**

1. The (students) came up with some good (ideas.)

2. _____

_____

3. _____

_____

4. _____

_____

Nouns as Objects

When you think of nouns, you probably think of them as the subjects of sentences. But nouns may also be used as **objects.** In the two sentences below, *dog* and *street* are objects. (Handbook page 420 explains nouns used as objects.)

Examples

The <u>cat</u> <u>chased</u> the *dog*.

The <u>ball</u> <u>rolled</u> into the *street*.

Directions Each sentence below has at least one noun used as an object. Underline and label each object: direct object, indirect object, or object of preposition. One example of each kind has been done for you.

    indirect object *direct object*

1. The teacher gave <u>Julie</u> a <u>pencil</u>.

      object of preposition

2. Mom parked behind the <u>school</u>.

3. Joey called the police.

4. We built a playhouse.

5. Mom painted our house.

6. Last night, I read Brad a story.

7. Rene gave Michael a cookie.

8. Darla sent me a valentine.

9. Gerardo gave a speech to our class.

10. Angel brought everyone an eraser.

The Next Step **Copy any three sentences from the previous page. Rewrite them so the noun that is now the subject of the sentence is used as an object in the new sentence. The first one has been done for you.**

1. **Original Sentence:** Joey called the police.

New Sentence: ___The police called Joey._____

2. **Original Sentence:** _____

_____

New Sentence: _____

_____

_____

3. **Original Sentence:** _____

_____

New Sentence: _____

_____

_____

4. **Original Sentence:** _____

_____

New Sentence: _____

_____

_____

Subject and Object Pronouns

A **pronoun** is a word used in place of a noun. A **subject pronoun** is used as the subject of a sentence. An **object pronoun** is used after an action verb or in a prepositional phrase. (See handbook page 423.)

Examples

  Subject Pronoun: We got lost.

  Object Pronoun: Mom and Dad found *us*.

| **Directions** | Each sentence below contains a subject pronoun, an object pronoun, or both. Underline each pronoun. Write *S* above each subject pronoun and *O* above each object pronoun. The first sentence has been done for you. |

1. $\overset{S}{\underline{We}}$ found $\overset{O}{\underline{them}}$ in the library.

2.   I left it at school.

3.   We helped her find the books.

4.   She needed them.

5.   After dessert, he read me a story.

6.   You saw us at the mall.

7.   He got a new sweater.

8.   It fits him.

9.   Yesterday, Paulo wrote me a note.

10.   The teacher saw it.

Directions   Cross out the complete subject of each sentence below. Replace the subject with the correct subject pronoun: *he, she, it,* or *they*. The first one has been done for you.

He
1. ~~Philip~~ likes bananas.

2. Jessica brought the cake.

3. The weather is too cold for Harry.

4. Tim and Charlie know Michelle.

5. Last night, my parents met my teacher and her husband.

6. The house belongs to Ms. Rojas.

7. After school, Jeff walked home with Sue.

8. The cat belongs to Juanita.

9. Elena found the book for Jose.

10. Mr. Montoya listened to the band students practice.

11. The close game got the fans excited.

12. Erika and Laura wrapped the present.

13. Michelle forgot to call her parents.

14. John ate the hot fudge sundae.

15. Six students helped decorate the stage.

The Next Step   **Now cross out each noun or noun phrase in the above sentence and write the correct object pronoun (*him, her, it,* or *them*) above it.**

Possessive Pronouns

A **possessive pronoun** shows ownership. (See handbook page 423.)

Examples

We wrote *our* poems on the board.

Mine was the shortest.

Yours was the funniest.

| **Directions** | Underline the possessive pronouns in the following sentences. The first sentence has been done for you. |

1. <u>Our</u> teacher read <u>my</u> poem.

2. The fifth graders had their field trip today.

3. The fourth grade has its field trip next week.

4. Which softball is ours, and which is theirs?

5. Did you bring your glove?

6. No, but Buddy brought his.

7. He brought his bats, too.

8. My brother is watching our jackets for us.

9. Is that my glass, or yours?

10. That's her glass; this one is yours.

11. I thought the other one was hers!

12. The one that's full is mine.

The Next Step **Replace each underlined word or phrase below with a possessive pronoun. The first one has been done for you.**

                                                    his
1   On the way to school, Jeremy dropped <u>Jeremy's</u> backpack in

2   a big puddle of slush. All of <u>Jeremy's</u> books, papers, markers,

3   and everything got soaked. When the teacher collected homework,

4   Jeremy handed <u>Jeremy's</u> homework in—still dripping! When

5   Jeremy needed a pen, he asked Alicia if he could borrow

6   <u>Alicia's pen</u>. Of course, he needed paper, too, so he asked Mark

7   for some of <u>Mark's paper</u>. When he needed a dry math book,

8   he asked me if he could share <u>my math book</u>. At lunch,

9   Jeremy needed dry food! Hannah and Todd let Jeremy share

10   <u>Hannah's and Todd's</u> sandwiches. Tina and I told Jeremy that

11   if he wanted some raw carrots, he could have <u>our raw carrots</u>.

12   Jeremy said, "Thanks, Jim, but I'd rather eat <u>Jeremy's</u> wet

13   cookies than <u>Tina's and Jim's</u> dry carrots."

14   Tina gave some of <u>Tina's</u> dessert to Jeremy. I gave him

15   a banana and said, "Sorry, buddy, but this brownie is all

16   <u>my brownie</u>!"

Personal Pronouns Review

A **subject pronoun** is used as the subject of a sentence. An **object pronoun** is used *after* an action verb or *in* a prepositional phrase. A **possessive pronoun** shows ownership. (To learn more about each of these pronouns, carefully read the sample sentences and the information about personal pronouns on handbook page 423.)

Directions	Turn to handbook page 99 and read the sample essay "Talent Show and Tell." With a partner, search for personal pronouns in the essay. *In the order in which you find them,* write the pronouns in the correct box below. *Hint:* There are 20 personal pronouns in the model.

Subject Pronouns

Singular	
Plural	

Object Pronouns

Singular	
Plural	

Possessive Pronouns

Singular	
Plural	

The Next Step Write a paragraph about something your school is proud of. Trade paragraphs with a classmate and circle all of your partner's pronouns. Then put each pronoun into the correct box below. Return the papers to each other and check each other's work.

_____

_____

_____

_____

_____

_____

_____

Subject Pronouns

Singular	
Plural	

Object Pronouns

Singular	
Plural	

Possessive Pronouns

Singular	
Plural	

Indefinite Pronouns

An **indefinite pronoun** does not name the word it replaces. (See the bottom of handbook page 424 for a list of indefinite pronouns.)

Examples

Several forgot their lunches.

Each of them bought a snack in the cafeteria.

Directions Underline the indefinite pronouns in the following sentences. (Some sentences have more than one indefinite pronoun.)

1. Someone left all of these books here.

2. Nobody knows who did it.

3. Some of us have finished our projects.

4. Most of us did all of our homework.

5. Everybody is going to the library.

6. In the end, everything turned out fine.

7. Both of my brothers are older than I am.

8. None of us remembered to bring anything to drink.

9. Each of us was supposed to bring something.

10. Does anyone want another dessert?

11. Many of the students walk to school.

Directions	An indefinite pronoun is a bit mysterious; it does not name the word it replaces. That means that indefinite pronouns are right at home in a mystery story! Write five sentences that sound as if they were taken from a mystery story. Use at least one indefinite pronoun in each sentence. Two examples have been done for you.

1. Suddenly, <u>everyone</u> was silent.

2. <u>No one</u> knew who had unlocked the cage and let the cobra

escape.

3. _____

_____

4. _____

_____

5. _____

_____

6. _____

_____

7. _____

_____

Person of a Pronoun

The **person of a pronoun** tells you whether the pronoun represents a person who is speaking, a person who is being spoken to, or a person or thing that is being spoken about. (See handbook page 422.)

Examples

	First-Person Pronoun	Second-Person Pronoun	Third-Person Pronoun
	Represents Person Speaking	Represents Person Being Spoken To	Represents Person or Thing Being Spoken About
Singular	**I**	**you**	**he, she, it**
Plural	**we**	**you**	**they**

Directions In the sentences below, fill in each blank with the correct pronoun from the table above. The first one has been done for you.

1   _____*I*_____ have a friend named Jerry who went out on a

2   boat to see whales in the ocean. _____ have to come to the

3   surface to breathe. Jerry said _____ saw four whales.

4   _____ said _____ slap their tails on the water, just for

5   fun. _____ said that one whale was so close to the boat

6   that when _____ slapped its tail, water splashed on him.

7   A whale expert named Tasha was on the boat. _____

8   told Jerry that whales eat one ton of food every day.

9   _____ told Jerry I didn't believe it. _____ answered,

10 "If _____ saw how big _____ are, you'd believe it!"

Directions In the following sentences, the personal pronouns are underlined. Write a *1* above each first-person pronoun, a *2* above each second-person pronoun, and a *3* above each third-person pronoun. The first sentence has been done for you.

    3   *1*   *1*   *3*
1. He likes me, and I like him.

2. Do you want to go sledding with me?

3. We had hot cocoa, and they built a snowman.

4. They put a hat on its head.

5. Where did you and he go?

6. Is she going with you or with me?

7. You and I should go in their car.

8. They don't know where his house is.

9. She borrowed the sled from him because he wasn't using it.

10. You can return it to us or to them.

11. Is our sled in your car or in their car?

12. We could put our toboggan on the roof of the van if it fits.

Pronoun-Antecedent Agreement

The pronouns in your sentences must agree with their antecedents. An **antecedent** is the name for the noun that a pronoun replaces. (See handbook page 421.)

Examples

Rod's *sister* lost *her* sunglasses at the beach.
(The pronoun *her* and the word it replaces, *sister,* are both singular, so they agree.)

Angie and Julie go body surfing whenever *they* can.
(The pronoun *they* and the words it replaces, *Angie and Julie,* are both plural, so they agree.)

Directions	Circle the pronouns in each of the following sentences. Draw an arrow to each pronoun's antecedent. If a pronoun does not agree with this antecedent, cross it out and write the correct pronoun above it. The first one has been done for you.

1. Rod and Angie got up early so ~~she~~ *they* could go on the tide-pool walk.

2. The naturalist told the group of early-morning hikers to follow them.

3. People wore rain gear because they were told to expect rain on the

   Olympic coast.

4. As the sun rose over the Olympic Mountains, they created a foggy,

   golden glow.

5. Rod slipped on the tide-pool rocks that had seaweed growing on it.

6. Tentacles coming from the sea anemones made it look like flowers

   to Angie.

7. One deep-orange starfish lifted an arm as it moved across a rock in

slow motion.

8. Empty sea urchin shells were scattered about where seagulls left them.

9. The yellow sea slugs crossing the pool looked like it needed a rest.

10. Angie liked barnacles that they thought looked like jumping jacks.

11. As the tide started coming in, Rod called for Angie to wait for him.

12. Then the tide pools disappeared; they will reappear at the next low tide.

The Next Step   **Write two pairs of sentences. In the first sentence, use a noun. In the second sentence of each pair, use a pronoun that agrees with the antecedent in your first sentence.**

1. _____

_____

2. _____

_____

1. _____

_____

2. _____

_____

Types of Verbs 1

There are three types of **verbs.** (See handbook pages 425-426.) **Action verbs** tell what the subject is doing. **Linking verbs** link a subject to a noun or an adjective. **Helping verbs** help state an action or show time.

Examples

Action Verbs: ran, jumped

Linking Verbs: was, seemed

Helping Verbs: has been, will

| **Directions** | Write down as many examples of each type of verb as you can in 8 minutes! When your time is up, use the explanations in your handbook to check your verbs. |

Action Verbs	**Linking Verbs**	**Helping Verbs**
_____	_____	_____
_____	_____	_____
_____	_____	_____
_____	_____	_____
_____	_____	_____
_____	_____	_____
_____	_____	_____
_____	_____	_____

The Next Step Write a story about preparing and eating your favorite food. Underline and label the verbs in your story: *A* (action), *L* (linking), or *H* (helping). Share your work with a classmate.

_____

_____

_____

_____

_____

_____

_____

_____

_____

_____

_____

_____

_____

Types of Verbs 2

There are three types of verbs: **action verbs,** **linking verbs,** and **helping verbs.** (They're explained on handbook pages 425-426.)

Examples

    Action Verbs: watch, swam

    Linking Verbs: is, appear

    Helping Verbs: are, have been

Directions	All the verbs in the following story are underlined. Label each verb *action, linking,* or *helping.* Two of them have been labeled for you.

         action   *helping*

1   "Get down, Antonio. They will see you. Get down."

2   Everything was happening so fast. Captain Magellan was

3   dead, the crew had scattered into the woods, and now we were

4   under attack.

5   "Juan," whispered Antonio. "Since the captain is dead, you

6   are now in charge. You must get us out of here."

7   Yes, Antonio was right. I, Juan Sebastian del Cano, was in

8   charge. But get us out of here? How?

9   There was no chance that we would survive if we stayed

10   on the ship. Escaping, as the crew had done, was our only hope.

11   "Antonio," I said, "we will swim for it."

The Next Step Continue the story about Antonio and Juan Sebastian del Cano. What will happen to them? Where will they go? Afterward, underline and label the verbs: *A* (action), *L* (linking), or *H* (helping). Share your work with a classmate.

_____

_____

_____

_____

_____

_____

_____

_____

_____

_____

_____

_____

_____

_____

_____

Singular and Plural Verbs

A **singular verb** must be used when the subject in a sentence is singular. A **plural verb** must be used when the subject is plural. (See handbook page 428.)

Examples

Singular Verbs: talks, gives, clucks

Plural Verbs: talk, give, cluck

| **Directions** | Give a name to each of the children below. Then write a sentence about each of them, using one of these singular verbs: *looks, wishes, waits, hopes, stares, listens, wonders, tries, keeps, sees,* and *smiles.* The first one has been done for you. |

1. Marty stares at the hamster in the cage.

_____

2. _____

_____

3. _____

_____

4. _____

_____

_____

5. _____

_____

Marty

_____

_____

The Next Step **Write three sentences with the word *children* as the subject. Use one of these plural verbs in each of your sentences: *wonder, hope,* and *see.***

1. _____

_____

_____

2. _____

_____

_____

3. _____

_____

_____

Verb Tenses

Verb tenses tell the time of a verb. (See handbook page 427.) The **present tense** of a verb describes something that is happening now or something that happens regularly. The **past tense** of a verb describes something that happened in the past. The **future tense** of a verb describes something that will happen in the future.

Examples

Present Tense: The bear <u>eats</u>.

Past Tense: The bear <u>ate</u>.

Future Tense: The bear <u>will eat</u>.

Directions   Circle the present tense verb in each sentence below. Then, on the lines after each sentence, write the verb in the past tense and the future tense. The first sentence has been done for you.

	Past Tense	Future Tense
1. I (play) my stereo at top volume.	*played*	*will play*
2. I sing along.	_____	_____
3. But no one hears me.	_____	_____
4. The stereo is too loud.	_____	_____
5. My brother goes nuts.	_____	_____
6. My mother rolls her eyes.	_____	_____
7. My father laughs.	_____	_____
8. Our dog Elvis howls.	_____	_____
9. Our cat Joe Bob runs away.	_____	_____

The Next Step List three verbs below. (You can pick three from the list on page 429 of your handbook, or you can use any other verbs.) Have a classmate do the same thing; then trade lists. For each of the three verbs you receive, write three sentences. Use the *present tense* of the verb in one sentence, the *past tense* in another sentence, and the *future tense* in your last sentence.

Three Verbs:

1. _____

2. _____

3. _____

Present Tense Sentences:

1. _____

2. _____

3. _____

Past Tense Sentences:

1. _____

2. _____

3. _____

Future Tense Sentences:

1. _____

2. _____

3. _____

Irregular Verbs 1

To make most verbs past tense, you simply add "ed" to the end. Easy. But then there are **irregular verbs.** They're called irregular because you don't make them past tense in the regular way. (For a list of irregular verbs, see handbook page 429.)

Examples

Irregular Verbs: ride, rode, ridden
run, ran, run
set, set, set

Directions   **Study the chart of irregular verbs on page 429. Then close your handbook and fill in the missing words in the chart below.**

present tense	past tense	past participle
1. break	_____	*(have) broken*
2. bring	_____	_____
3. come	*came*	_____
4. drink	_____	*(have) drunk*
5. know	*knew*	_____
6. lead	_____	_____
7. shake	_____	*(have) shaken*
8. sing	_____	*(have) sung*
9. speak	*spoke*	_____
10. take	_____	_____

Irregular Verbs 2

This exercise gives you practice using **irregular verbs.** (Before you begin, review the chart of irregular verbs on handbook page 429.)

Examples

Irregular Verbs: see, saw, seen
sit, sat, sat
burst, burst, burst

| **Directions** | In each sentence below, fill in the blank with the correct form of the verb that appears in parentheses. Try this without looking at your handbook. The first sentence has been done for you. |

1. The rain _____froze_____ and made the streets slick. *(freeze)*

2. Our cat's water was _____ , too. *(freeze)*

3. My uncle _____ me to a museum last week. *(take)*

4. He has _____ me to a lot of fun places. *(take)*

5. I _____ up at 7:00 a.m. yesterday. *(wake)*

6. I _____ my bike to my cousin's house. *(ride)*

7. I had never _____ there before. *(ride)*

8. Misha was _____ by a spider. *(bite)*

9. The spider _____ him on the foot. *(bite)*

10. His neighbor _____ over to look at it. *(come)*

11. Misha's mom _____ to the doctor. *(speak)*

Irregular Verbs Review

This activity gives you more practice with irregular verbs.

Directions	To practice using irregular verbs, change the underlined verbs to the past tense. The first sentence has been done for you.

1   The doorbell ~~rings~~ *rang*. I <u>wake</u> up. It <u>is</u> Saturday morning, and

2   the snow <u>is</u> coming down hard. My uncle <u>stands</u> outside our door

3   with a huge package, taller than I am. He <u>brings</u> the package

4   inside. A freezing wind <u>blows</u> in. With a wink and a smile, he

5   <u>says</u> the present <u>is</u> for me. It <u>isn't</u> my birthday or anything. He

6   <u>sets</u> it in the hallway. "Don't open it yet," he <u>says</u>. "What's for

7   breakfast?" I <u>eat</u> in a hurry. My uncle <u>drinks</u> coffee and <u>talks</u> to

8   my mom. I <u>steal</u> glances at the package. I <u>fight</u> the urge to run

9   to the hallway and open it. Finally my uncle <u>says</u>, "Well, I guess

10 it's time!" I <u>run</u> to the hallway. I <u>shake</u> the box—it <u>is</u> not heavy

11 at all for such a big box. I <u>lay</u> it on its side. I <u>tear</u> off the

12 wrapping paper. At the bottom of the box, something <u>shines</u> like

13 silver . . . silver with a long wooden handle. It <u>is</u> a snow shovel!

14 My uncle <u>bursts</u> out laughing. "Let it snow, let it snow, let it

15 snow!" he <u>sings</u>. I <u>begin</u> to plan my revenge, but then my uncle

16 <u>makes</u> it up to me: He <u>takes</u> me to the movies.

The Next Step **For a challenge, write your own paragraph using lots of irregular verbs in the present tense. Then trade paragraphs with a partner, and change each other's verbs to the past tense.**

_____

_____

_____

_____

_____

_____

_____

_____

_____

_____

_____

_____

_____

_____

Subject-Verb Agreement 1

Subject-verb agreement basically means that if the subject of a sentence is singular, the verb must be singular, too; if the subject is plural, the verb must be plural, too. (See handbook pages 116 and 412-413.)

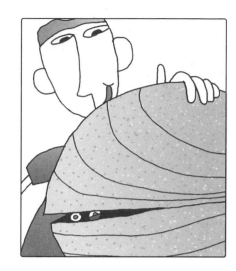

Examples

Singular Subject and Verb:
Sheila has a chinchilla.

Plural Subject and Verb:
The students in our class have strange pets.

| **Directions** | In the sentences below, cross out the incorrect verb and write the correct one on the line provided. The verb you choose should agree with the subject. The first sentence has been done for you. |

1. Two students in our class ~~has~~ iguanas.   *have*

2. Jamila have a ferret.   _____

3. Ferrets is a lot like weasels.   _____

4. Jamila's ferret are named Gizmo.   _____

5. He run really fast.   _____

6. Jamila's golden retriever Sam love Gizmo.   _____

7. They takes naps together.   _____

8. Gizmo sneak up on Sam sometimes.   _____

9. Then he bite Sam's ears.   _____

10. He are just playing, though.   _____

The Next Step **Write five sentences about an unusual or an imaginary pet. Make sure the subjects and verbs of your sentences "agree." Then trade papers with a classmate and check each other's work.**

1. _____

_____

_____

2. _____

_____

_____

3. _____

_____

_____

4. _____

_____

_____

5. _____

_____

_____

Subject-Verb Agreement 2

This activity gives you practice making subjects and verbs "agree" in sentences that have compound subjects.   There are two basic rules you need to know:

1. A compound subject connected by **and** needs a plural verb.

2. A compound subject connected by **or** may need a plural or a singular verb. The verb must agree with the subject that is closer to it.

Note: See handbook page 116 for examples.

| Directions | Using the rules above, correct the following sentences by making the subject and verb agree. At the end of each sentence, write which rule you used. The first two have been done for you. |

1. Michelle and Cindy ~~is~~ *are* going to start a band. *(Use rule 1.)*

2. Either the cats or the dog ~~have~~ *has* to go out. *(Use rule 2.)*
   The verb agrees with dog, the closer subject.

3. Either Tom or Marsha play shortstop.

4. Dan and Amy takes guitar lessons.

5. Chachi and Cindy is the best singers in our school.

6. Cindy's brothers or sister usually sing with her.

7. Charlie's brother or sisters is always yelling at him.

8. Jeff and Darla goes to California every summer.

9. Sue's brothers and cousin plays tennis.

10. Sue's brothers or cousin are coming to pick her up.

The Next Step   **Using the rules on the previous page, write two sentences that fit rule number 1 and two that fit rule number 2. Exchange papers with a classmate and check each other's subject-verb agreement.**

Rule 1:

1. _____

_____

_____

2. _____

_____

_____

Rule 2:

1. _____

_____

_____

2. _____

_____

_____

Subject-Verb Agreement Review

This activity gives you practice with subject-verb agreement.

Directions | **Some of the underlined verbs below do not agree with their subjects. If the verb does not agree, cross it out and write the correct verb above it. If the verb does agree, put a check mark above it. The first two have been done for you.**

1   My brother and sisters ~~is~~ *are* all teenagers. I <u>have</u> ✓ learned from

2   them that teenagers <u>is</u> weird. For one thing, they <u>does</u> strange

3   things to their hair. You never <u>know</u> what my sisters or my

4   brother <u>are</u> going to do next. First, Kenny <u>bleaches</u> his hair; then

5   he <u>shave</u> his head. When his hair <u>starts</u> to grow again, he <u>look</u>

6   scary. Meanwhile, my sisters <u>starts</u> out with brown hair. They

7   <u>looks</u> fine. Then one day Kelly <u>have</u> blonde hair, and Kendra

8   <u>have</u> red hair. The next week, Kelly <u>is</u> a redhead, and Kendra

9   <u>are</u> a blonde. Sometimes they even <u>add</u> stripes—blue, yellow, or

10   red. My brother or my sisters <u>is</u> always in the bathroom doing

11   things to their hair. Sometimes they <u>tries</u> to put things on my

12   hair, and I <u>have</u> to scream for help. I <u>tell</u> my mom I <u>are</u> not

13   going to be a teenager. She <u>say</u>, "That <u>is</u> okay with me. Your

14   sisters and your brother <u>is</u> enough teenagers in one house."

The Next Step In the space provided below, draw a cartoon about teenagers. Write a caption for your cartoon. Make sure your subjects and verbs agree. (A caption is a sentence that tells what is happening in the picture, as in the following example.)

Example

New mousse, Bill?

Your Cartoon:

Adjectives

An **adjective** is a word that describes a noun or a pronoun. Sometimes more than one adjective is used to describe one word. (See handbook pages 430-431 for more about adjectives; see page 380 for information about using commas to separate adjectives.)

Examples

Realistic fiction is fun to read.

Beverly Cleary writes *funny, entertaining* books.

| Directions | Think about a book of fiction that you have read. Then, in the chart below, write the names of the main character and one other character, and as many adjectives as you can think of to describe each. |

Book Title: _____

		Adjectives
The Main Character		
One Other Character		

The Next Step   **Now write a descriptive paragraph about one of the characters you described on the previous page. Use adjectives from your chart.**

_____

_____

_____

_____

_____

_____

_____

_____

_____

_____

_____

_____

_____

_____

Forms of Adjectives

The **positive form** of an adjective describes a noun without comparing it to anyone or anything else. The **comparative form** of an adjective compares two people, places, things, or ideas. The **superlative form** compares three or more people, places, things, or ideas. (See handbook page 430.)

Examples

Positive:	Miguel is a *fast* runner.
Comparative:	He is *faster* than anyone else on the team.
Superlative:	He is the *fastest* runner in the league.

Positive:	Sylvia is a *skillful* skateboarder.
Comparative:	She is *more skillful* now than she was last year.
Superlative:	She is now the *most skillful* skateboarder on her block. (*More* and *most*, not *er* and *est,* are usually used with adjectives of two or more syllables.)

Directions   **Write three sentences about your favorite sport. Use the three forms of an adjective, one in each sentence.**

1. _____

    _____

    _____

2. _____

    _____

    _____

3. _____

    _____

The Next Step Write a paragraph about the best or worst experience you have had in sports. You may use some of the sentences you wrote in the first part of this activity. Be sure to use the positive, comparative, and superlative forms of adjectives.

_____

_____

_____

_____

_____

_____

_____

_____

_____

_____

_____

_____

_____

Colorful Adjectives

Colorful adjectives appeal to your senses and add life to your writing. (Check out "Choose colorful modifiers" on handbook page 66.)

Examples

Sight: the *dazzling* lights

Sound: a *screaming* siren

Smell: the *sour* odor of spoiled milk

Taste: the *fiery* jalapeño pepper

Feel: *scratchy* cloth

Directions	In the sentences below, fill in each blank with an adjective. Use colorful adjectives that tell the reader how things looked, sounded, smelled, tasted, and so on.

1   My cousin took me to a carnival. It was nighttime, and the

2   moon was _____ . The _____

3   carnival lights glowed. _____ music was playing.

4   The _____ smell of popcorn was in the air. I could hear

5   the _____ screams of people on the _____

6   roller coaster. I wanted to ride it, but I felt unsure. My heart

7   pounded as I watched the _____ roller-coaster cars

8   plunge down the track. My _____ cousin said, "Let's

9   go, kid." We got on. Our _____ car lurched forward.

10 I gripped the bar tightly with _____ hands.

11   We chugged up a steep section of track. From the top, the whole

12   carnival looked _____ and _____ .

13   Suddenly, we were falling. I screamed and closed my eyes.

The Next Step **Write a "sensory poem" about a time you went on a roller coaster or some other ride. In a sensory poem, you have to use details that describe sights, sounds, feelings, smells, and tastes. (See handbook page 256 for more details.)**

_____

_____

_____

_____

_____

_____

_____

_____

_____

_____

Adverbs

An **adverb** is a word that describes a verb, an adjective, or another adverb. Most adverbs answer when, where, or how questions. (See handbook page 432.)

Example

Describing a Verb:
The kindergartners go *annually* to a farm.

Directions	In the following sentences about field trips, circle the adverbs and underline the verbs they describe. The first sentence has been done for you. *Hint:* Sometimes more than one adverb in the same sentence can describe the same word.

1. The first-grade class (always) takes a trip to the zoo (early) in the fall.

2. Sometimes the second-grade class visits a local farm to pick apples.

3. The third grade usually travels down to the natural history museum and then writes a class report about endangered species.

4. Surprisingly, the fourth grade often votes for a field day to clean up the vacant lots in the neighborhood.

5. The fifth-grade class happily goes away to science camp for three days in the spring.

6. The sixth graders proudly march in the Earth Day parade.

7. In seventh grade, the students greatly enjoy the planetarium's special show about stars, comets, and the planets.

Directions Now put the adverbs you just found into the circles that answer the following questions for each verb. The adverbs from the first sentence have been listed for you.

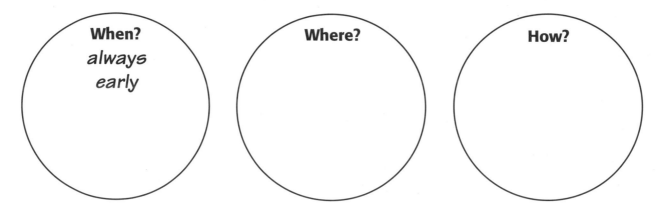

When?
always
early

Where?

How?

The Next Step Sometimes things that weren't planned happen on field trips. Can you remember a surprising incident from a field trip? Write about it. Start your story with the adverb *surprisingly*. Then share your story with your class.

_____

_____

_____

_____

_____

_____

_____

_____

Forms of Adverbs

There are three forms of adverbs: the **positive** form, the **comparative** form, and the **superlative** form. (See page 433 in your handbook. Make sure to note the special forms for *well* and *badly*.)

Examples

Positive:
I run *swiftly* and jump *high.*

Comparative:
He runs *more swiftly* and jumps *higher.*

Superlative:
She runs *most swiftly* and jumps *highest.*

| **Directions** | In each sentence, fill in the blanks with the correct forms of the adverb in *boldface.* The first sentence has been done for you. |

1. Zoe did **well** on the test, but Jolene did _____*better*_____ , and

   Bianca did _____*best*_____ .

2. Jerry talks **fast,** but Yolanda talks _____ , and

   Laurie talks _____ .

3. We did **badly** in the race, but Mike's team did _____ ,

   and Georgia's team did _____ .

4. Rolly swims **well,** but Lamarr swims _____ , and

   Felix swims _____ .

5. Angela climbed **carefully,** but Gary climbed _____ ,

   and Eric climbed _____ .

6. John studies **hard,** but Sharon studies _____ , and

   Tomas studies _____ .

7. Joanne speaks **clearly,** but Fumiko speaks_____ , and

   Sam speaks _____ .

8. Paloma sings **beautifully,** but Elena sings _____ , and

   Susan sings _____ .

Directions	Fill in the comparative and superlative forms of the following adverbs. Then write sentences using all three forms of each adverb. (See handbook page 433 for help.)

Positive Form	Comparative Form	Superlative Form
badly		
bravely		
late		
well		

1. (badly) _____

   _____

2. (bravely) _____

   _____

3. (late) _____

   _____

4. (well) _____

   _____

Prepositions

A **preposition** always "pulls" other words behind it, like a train engine pulling boxcars. A prepositional phrase is the whole train—a preposition plus the words it "pulls along." (See handbook page 434.)

Example

Take a Walk in Their Shoes is a great book!
(The word *in* is a preposition; the words *in Their Shoes* is a prepositional phrase.)

Directions | Each book title below contains one preposition. Circle each preposition, and underline the words it pulls along. The first one has been done for you.

1. (About) the B'Nai Bagels

2. Among the Volcanoes

3. A Blessing in Disguise

4. Boys at Work

5. Bridge to Terabithia

6. Fat Men from Space

7. Journey into Terror

8. Little House on the Prairie

9. Sees Behind Trees

10. Miracle at the Plate

11. Sybil Rides for Independence

12. Tales of a Fourth Grade Nothing

13. A Letter to Amy

14. When I Was Young in the Mountains

15. Song of the Trees

16. Arthur for the Very First Time

17. On the Riverbank

18. Sweet Rhymes Around the World

19. Sideways Stories from Wayside School

20. If You Grew Up with George Washington

The Next Step **Write down five more book titles that have prepositions. These can be titles of real books or titles you make up. Circle the prepositions and underline the words that are pulled along to make up a prepositional phrase.**

1. _____

_____

2. _____

_____

3. _____

_____

4. _____

_____

5. _____

_____

Interjections

An **interjection** is a word or phrase used to express strong emotion or surprise. A comma or an exclamation point is used to separate an interjection from the rest of the sentence. (See handbook page 433.)

Examples

Yikes! The cat's in the top tree branches!

Did you hear that motorcycle? *Wow!*

Watch where you're going, *hey*!

Man, that's dangerous!

Directions Pretend you are talking on the phone to your friend. At the same time, pretend you look out the window and see something surprising. Choose one of the sentences above as a starting point for writing a story. Tell your friend about what you are observing. Use a variety of interjections and short sentences to describe what you "see" from the window.

_____

_____

_____

_____

_____

_____

_____

_____

Conjunctions

Conjunctions are connecting words. (The kinds of conjunctions are explained on handbook page 435.)

Examples

Coordinating Conjunction:
The wind stopped, *so* I couldn't fly my kite.

Subordinating Conjunction:
I couldn't fly my kite *after* the wind stopped.

Directions   **Use conjunctions to connect the following sentences. You may have to make some changes in wording to make your new sentence read smoothly and correctly. The kind of conjunction you should use is written in parentheses. (See handbook pages 121 and 435 for more about using conjunctions.)**

1. Robby went to class. Robby went to lunch. *(coordinating conjunction)*

    Robby went to class and to lunch.

2. I worked on my homework. I didn't finish it. *(coordinating conjunction)*

    _____

3. It was raining. The game was canceled. *(coordinating conjunction)*

    _____

4. I made my lunch. I went to school. *(subordinating conjunction)*

    _____

5. We stopped playing. It started raining. *(subordinating conjunction)*

    _____

6. We went to get pizza. The game was canceled. *(subordinating conjunction)*

    _____

Coordinating Conjunctions

A **coordinating conjunction** connects equal parts of a sentence: two or more words, two or more phrases, or two or more clauses. The coordinating conjunctions are *and, but, or, nor, for, so,* and *yet.* (See handbook page 435.)

Examples

Connecting Words: Mugs *and* Barney barked.

Connecting Phrases: Kat ran out the door *and* into the yard.

Connecting Clauses: Kat kept running, *and* Mugs followed.

Directions   **Circle all the coordinating conjunctions in the following paragraph.**

1   When I was little, I was scared of the dark. I thought

2   monsters or ghosts would come out and yell, "Boo!" I imagined

3   closets hiding goblins or wild animals. Finally, I got a night-light,

4   and it worked like a charm. It was shaped like a seashell, and I

5   could see its friendly glow in the dark. It lit up my room a little,

6   so I could sleep better. Through the years, I enjoyed having my

7   night-light right next to my bed. Now I am older, and I don't

8   need it anymore.

Directions On the center of the lines below, copy some of the coordinating conjunctions you circled. On either side, write the words, phrases, or clauses that each conjunction connects. Two have been done for you.

1. _____

2. _____

3. ___ *I got a night-light*   *and*   *that worked like a charm.* ___

4. ___ *It lit up my room a little*   *so*   *I could sleep better.* ___

5. _____

The Next Step Choose another student sample from your handbook or something from your own writing folder. Find five phrases or clauses that contain coordinating conjunctions and write them here.

1. _____

2. _____

3. _____

4. _____

5. _____

Subordinating Conjunctions

A **subordinating conjunction** connects two clauses to make a complex sentence. The subordinating conjunction may come at the beginning or in the middle of the sentence. (See handbook page 435.)

Examples

After we went to the game, we stopped for ice cream.

We stopped for ice cream *after* we went to the game.

Directions　　Circle the subordinating conjunction in each sentence below. The first one has been done for you.

1. (Because) I missed the bus, I was late for school.

2. We play soccer in this park after school lets out.

3. We'll have to go inside if we see lightning.

4. We can't go swimming until the rain stops.

5. I won't finish my homework unless I start soon.

6. While I clean our room, Polly will walk the dog.

7. When I finish my homework, I'll call Sam.

8. Juanita couldn't come to school because she is sick.

9. Since it is dark, I don't want to walk home alone.

10. I like my aunt because she is funny.

11. Before we moved, I went to a different school.

| Directions | From the previous exercise, choose two sentences that have subordinating conjunctions at the beginning. Rewrite each sentence so the subordinating conjunction is in the middle. |

Examples

Because I missed the bus, I was late for school.

I was late for school *because* I missed the bus.

1. _____

_____

2. _____

_____

| Directions | Now choose two sentences that have subordinating conjunctions in the middle. Rewrite each sentence so the subordinating conjunction is at the beginning. |

1. _____

_____

2. _____

_____

Conjunctions Review

This activity is a review of coordinating and subordinating conjunctions.

Directions   **Each sentence below has one coordinating conjunction and one subordinating conjunction. Underline both, and write *C* above each coordinating conjunction and *S* above each subordinating conjunction. The first sentence has been done for you.**

1. My sister <u>and</u> I washed our dog <u>after</u> he rolled in the mud.

2. We could play basketball or go roller-skating unless it's too cold.

3. Jerry has to change clothes and clean his room before he can play.

4. We went to the mall, yet we couldn't find the store where we had seen the video game.

5. Though it was almost time for dinner, we ate cookies and brownies.

6. We're not hungry, but we'll eat if you're having pizza!

7. Stephanie and I walked to the museum after we rode the bus downtown.

8. Jim or Amir can feed the fish while Sandy waters the plants.

9. I want to watch TV, but I can't unless I finish my homework.

10. Because it's raining, my mom or dad will pick me up.

11. Although Heather had a cat, she still wanted a parakeet and a lovebird.

12. After my birthday party, I wanted to write and send all my thank-you notes by e-mail.

The Next Step **Add the needed conjunctions to the sentences below. Then write three sentences of your own in which you use and underline conjunctions.**

1. _____ it's 9:00, Lilly _____ James are still sleeping.

2. It's Tuesday, _____ practice is canceled _____ it's raining.

3. My dad honked the horn, _____ the cow stayed in the road

   _____ another car came along.

4. _____

   _____

   _____

5. _____

   _____

   _____

6. _____

   _____

   _____

Parts of Speech Review 1

This activity is a review of all the parts of speech you have studied. Do the activity with a partner if your teacher allows it.

Each list below contains words that are examples of one part of speech. Label each list with the name of the correct part of speech.

_____	_____	_____
dog	run	I
book	said	you
California	throw	their
idea	write	his
mechanic	were	anyone

_____	_____	_____
quickly	big	of
loudly	tall	at
well	tallest	to
carefully	smart	over
down	an	on top of

_____	_____
Hey!	and
Oh!	or
Wow!	but
Yikes!	because
Yes!	although

Directions	Read the following fable. Above each underlined word, write the correct part of speech. The first two have been done for you.

The Farmer and the Sticks

1   Long ago, there was a <u>farmer</u> who had many sons <u>and</u>
                                    noun   *conjunction*

2   daughters. <u>His</u> children were always fighting <u>with</u> one another.

3   One day, the farmer had a clever idea. He took a bunch of <u>small</u>

4   sticks and <u>tied</u> them together like one big <u>log</u>. Then he

5   challenged each of his children to try to break the bundle in two.

6   Each one tried <u>hard</u>, but <u>they</u> all failed. Then the farmer

7   carefully untied the bundle. He <u>asked</u> each child to try to break

8   one of the sticks. Of course, they all did it <u>easily</u>. Then the <u>wise</u>

9   farmer said, "Do <u>you</u> see? If you all stick together, no one can

10   harm you, <u>but</u> alone, you can easily be destroyed!"

Parts of Speech Review 2

This activity is a review of all the parts of speech you have studied.

Directions   **Read the following fable. Above each underlined word, write the correct part of speech. The first two have been done for you.**

The Ant and the Dove

1   One _day_, an ant _crawled_ to a little pond to have a drink.

noun above "day", _verb_ above "crawled"

2   When _he_ was almost to the pond's edge, he _fell_ down the _slippery_

3   bank into the _water_. The ant was about to drown when a _dove_

4   _saw_ him. The dove _quickly_ dropped a _leaf_ into the pond. The ant

5   climbed onto the leaf and drifted _safely_ back to land. As he

6   _stepped_ off the leaf, the ant looked up _and_ saw a hunter taking

7   aim _at_ the dove. The _tiny_ ant bit the hunter hard on the heel.

8   The hunter said, "_Ouch!_" The dove heard _him_ and flew away. The

9   _moral_ of the story is "One good turn deserves another."

Directions Open your handbook to the first page of "Montgomery Mews Mysteriously" on pages 210-211. List examples of the parts of speech you find in the story.

Nouns | Verbs | Pronouns

_____ | _____ | _____

_____ | _____ | _____

_____ | _____ | _____

Adverbs | Adjectives | Prepositions

_____ | _____ | _____

_____ | _____ | _____

_____ | _____ |

Conjunctions | Interjections

_____ | _____